DATE DUE

NOV 12 1987	BIRD	NOV 5 1987 RET
MAR 21 1989		APR 25 1989 RET
JAN 10 1991	BIRD	
		DEC 5 REC'D

Demco, Inc. 38-293

S0-ESV-040

Television in Urban Education
Its Application to Major Educational Problems in Sixteen Cities

BALTIMORE
BOSTON
BUFFALO
CHICAGO

CLEVELAND
DETROIT
LOS ANGELES
MEMPHIS

MILWAUKEE
NEW YORK
PHILADELPHIA
PITTSBURGH

ST. LOUIS
SAN DIEGO
SAN FRANCISCO
WASHINGTON, D.C.

Introduction by
ALVA DITTRICK

The present study was conducted by The Fund for Media Research as part of the Educational Communications Project of the Research Council of the Great Cities Program for School Improvement, under a grant from the United States Office of Education.

The Research Council of the Great Cities Program for School Improvement consists of the Superintendents and one Board of Education member from each member city. Its purpose is "to conduct studies of unique problems faced by the Great Cities in their efforts to meet the comprehensive public school needs of their citizens."

SIDNEY P. MARLAND, JR.
President

EVERETT CHAFFEE
Chairman, Instructional Materials Committee

ROBERT R. SUCHY
Chairman, Instructional TV Subcommittee

CARL E. THORNBLAD
Executive Secretary; Project Director, Educational Communications Project

The Fund for Media Research was founded in April, 1967, as a nonprofit organization devoted to studies in education involving communications technology. Its primary commitment is to develop learning potential through educational media.

CHARLES W. BENTON
President

WAYNE K. HOWELL
Vice President

HUGH C. OPPENHEIMER
Vice President

HENRY H. URROWS
Research Consultant

PRAEGER SPECIAL STUDIES IN
U.S. ECONOMIC AND SOCIAL DEVELOPMENT

Television in Urban Education

Its Application to Major Educational Problems in Sixteen Cities

Charles W. Benton
Wayne K. Howell
Hugh C. Oppenheimer
Henry H. Urrows

Published in cooperation with
The Fund for Media Research

FREDERICK A. PRAEGER, Publishers
New York · Washington · London

The purpose of the Praeger Special Studies is to make specialized research monographs in U.S. and international economics and politics available to the academic, business, and government communities. For further information, write to the Special Projects Division, Frederick A. Praeger, Publishers, 111 Fourth Avenue, New York, N.Y. 10003.

FREDERICK A. PRAEGER, PUBLISHERS
111 Fourth Avenue, New York, N.Y. 10003, U.S.A.
5, Cromwell Place, London S.W.7, England

Published in the United States of America in 1969
by Frederick A. Praeger, Inc., Publishers

All rights reserved

© 1969 by Frederick A. Praeger, Inc.

Library of Congress Catalog Card Number: 68-58483

Printed in the United States of America

ACKNOWLEDGEMENTS

Only the unstinting efforts of many people made this Report possible. A list of "Persons Helpful to This Study" will be found in Appendix G. But the Report would be really incomplete without singling out certain people, whose help was indispensable to the success of this effort.

Too numerous to mention individually are all of the people in the Great Cities themselves, who were both the subjects of the Study and our principal guides. Especially important here are the Instructional Television Directors and Coordinators or people whom the Superintendents designated to coordinate our schedule and answer our questions in long interviews, by mail, and often over the telephone. On the overall coordination we are particularly grateful to Carl Thornblad and his staff at the Research Council.

For my first direct exposure to School Television at its best, I am grateful to Lew Rhodes, who was responsible for my visit to American Samoa last May with 10 Big-City Superintendents. Norton Kristy, Burt Wolin and Elias Porter of Technomics were especially helpful to us in reviewing our initial research framework and on the interpretation of our data. Claire List of the Ford Foundation helped us clarify the objectives, structure and wording of the report.

For help in design we are grateful to Mort Goldsholl of Goldsholl and Associates.

On the visual dimension of our report, the videotape of School Television excerpts and panel discussion, we are indebted to Robert Pirsein and his staff at New Trier Township Instructional Television and to Borden Mace of the Sterling Institute.

To keep us on the track financially and to help with the logistical aspects we are especially thankful to William Benton, Robert Morrison and the Continental Bank, Ozzie Kassin, our Accountant, Jack Wikoff, our landlord, and Lowell Sachnoff and Len Schrager of the law firm of Epstein, Manilow and Sachnoff.

Of course, all of this would not have been possible without the dedicated efforts of our office staff. Special thanks to our indefatigable Office Manager, Rhoda Wikoff, and the invisible but invaluable staff of secretaries and typists, including Sue Chattler, Kaye Randell, Michele Freeman, Pesh Clarke and Joanne Nesemeier.

Most importantly we are unendingly grateful for the understanding and support from our wives . . . whom we deserted while traveling to the 16 cities all summer long and without whose patience (stretched very far at times), the whole project would have ground to a halt.

For this sacrifice we are proud to dedicate our handiwork to:

Marge Benton
Terry Oppenheimer
Betty Urrows

Charles Benton

THE GREAT CITIES' PUBLIC SCHOOLS

Total Population ('60)	25,199,791	
White	19,890,438	(79%)
Non-white	5,309,353	(21%)
Public School Enrollment ('66-'67)	4,172,488	
White	2,189,180	(52%)
Non-white	1,983,308	(48%)
Public School Teachers ('66-'67)	174,941	
Expenditures for all School District Programs ('66-'67)	$3,389,647,303	
TV Budget ('66-'67)	$5,166,825	

Of the entire United States the 16 Great Cities have:

Population ('60)	
White	14.0%
Non-white	12.5
	25.9
Public School Enrollment ('66-'67)	
White	9.7
Non-white	6.1
	29.4
Classroom teachers	9.9
Expenditures of Public School Programs	12.6

If there were an average Great City it would have:

260,780	Pupils - Elem. & Sec.
48%	Non-white
10,934	Teachers
271	Buildings
$812.00	Expenditure per pupil
$211,952,956	Total Budget
$323,434	TV Budget

Some Relevant Facts in 1966-67:

New York had 92,786 non-English speaking students.
In five Detroit schools, pupil mobility reached 136%.
Washington, D.C. had 93% non-white students.
Three-fifths of all Chicago students were estimated to be from disadvantaged families.
In St. Louis, 70% of public school students live in poverty areas.

FOREWORD

The Research Council of the Great Cities commissioned The Fund for Media Research to examine the status and needs of the schools, as served by television, in member cities' public school systems.

Planned and completed in only a few months, mostly when the schools were not in regular session, the inquiry is a necessarily preliminary part of the wider series of inquiries on Educational Communications being conducted by the Research Council's Committee on Instructional Materials. The first phase of this project, on data processing, has already been done; a subsequent phase on instructional materials remains to be completed.

We precede the report by defining what the Council and the Fund undertook to do, and what this Study of television is not. Unlike several "major" studies undertaken in this decade — supervised by august overseeing committees, employing large staffs and numerous consultants, and taking years to complete, this Study was inexpensive. Its focus is upon what the cities and their Great Cities School Improvement Council can do.

Three principal investigators, with research and clerical assistance, first familiarized themselves with what other investigators had learned. They proceeded to find out what school people in our cities know and think. They encountered consistent responsiveness among 466 persons interviewed.

Their inquiry explores what school administrators, supervisors, curriculum specialists, principals, and teachers regard as the most acute instructional needs in the public schools of these cities; what the role of technology appears to be in helping meet these needs; what differing organizational structures exist in using Instructional Television; what cooperation is and is not being obtained among professional specialists with related responsibility; what Instructional Television series are being used at various grade levels and in diverse subject areas; what facilities exist and are felt to be needed for helping solve common, urgent problems.

This is not an appraisal of how well or how badly the school systems are doing their work. There are basic assumptions that each of our cities has a lot to be humble about, but we had better get on with the specific tasks that translate high purpose into constructive action. While a number of promising practices are identified, the objective is to do more, do it better, and do it sooner where cooperative effort can foster improved results in learning.

This is not a definitive critique on the state of the art of Instructional Television, even though commendations of certain activities are noted, and defects and inadequacies are reported. We were not out to bestow awards, nor booby prizes.

Nor is this study an impassioned essay on the familiar gaps between potentials and performance. It seeks to strengthen the Great Cities' ability to make informed judgments on what the Research Council can do to help narrow those gaps.

We believe that it also merits attention by those entrusted with the study of instructional television recommended by the Carnegie Commission on Educational Television, and the study called for by Title III of the Public Broadcasting Act.

While never intended to be comprehensive, this report is concerned with large and pressing questions directly affecting fully one-tenth of the students in U.S. public schools. Its findings, conclusions, and recommendations are presented as those of The Fund for Media Research.

S. P. Marland, Jr., President
Research Council of the Great
Cities Program for School Improvement

Charles W. Benton, President
The Fund for Media Research

CONTENTS

	Page
Acknowledgements	v
Foreword	vii
List of Figures and Map	xi
List of Tables	xii
Glossary	xiii
Introduction	xv

THE REPORT

I. THE GREAT CITIES' SCHOOL PROBLEMS

    1. Their Public School Systems 1

    2. Priority Instructional Problems 1

II. SCHOOL TELEVISION IN THE GREAT CITIES

    1. Programs and Uses 5

    2. Some Promising Practices 16

    3. Facilities and Operations 19

    4. Constraints 32

    5. Costs 34

    6. Summary of Findings 37

III. SUMMARY AND CONCLUSIONS 38

IV. RECOMMENDATIONS 39

APPENDICES

A.	Proposals and Suggestions Made by Great Cities' School People	45
B.	Excerpts from Interviews	47
C.	Charts on Instructional Problems and Persons Interviewed	63
D.	City by City Findings	73
E.	School Television Facilities and Personnel	111
F.	Statement on Public Broadcasting Act of 1967	123
G.	Persons and Sources Helpful to This Study	127
H.	School Television: Great Cities 1967 — A Discussion and Demonstration Videotape	131

BIBLIOGRAPHY 137

LIST OF FIGURES AND MAP

Figure		Page
1.*	The Cities' Most Acute Instructional Problems.	2
2.*	Most Acute Instructional Problems (By Cities).	3
3.*	The Most Acute Instructional Problems — As Seen By Persons with Different Professional Responsibilities.	4
4.	School Television Uses. Great Cities — 1966-67	6
5.	Percentage of Elementary & Secondary Enrollments Reported as Regular Users of ITV	8
6.	School Television Programming in the Great Cities, 1966-67 Compared with National Data For One Week in April, 1966 (By Grade Levels)	11
7.	School Television Broadcast Programming by Grade Level — Great Cities, 1966-67.	12
8.	Programming in the Great Cities, 1966-67 Compared with National Data for One Week in April, 1966	13
9.	Great Cities' School Television Broadcast Program Sources	15
10.	Television Receivers Per 500 Elementary Pupils.	27
11.	Television Receivers Per 500 Secondary Pupils.	29
12.	Deterrents To More Effective Use of Broadcast Television by City	31
13.	Percentage of Interview Responses on the Acute Instructional Problems — by Persons with Differing Professional Responsibilities.	68
14.	Curriculum Inadequacies	69
15.	Teacher Needs	70
16.	Interfering Environmental Realities	71
17.	Excessive Workload of Teachers.	72

Map		
1.	The Great Cities' Public Schools	vi

*Figures 1, 2 and 3 also appear in Appendix C.

LIST OF TABLES

Table		Page
A.	Percentage of Total School Hours for Which Instructional Television is Available	7
B.	Interviewees' "Guesstimates" of "Regular Users" of ITV	9
C.	Instructional Television Programming Distribution By Grade Levels (1966-67)	14
D.	Ownership of TV Channels Used By Great Cities' Schools 1966-67	20
E.	Original Broadcast Programming Comparative Output By Cities — 1966-67	23
F.	Reported Budgeted Expenditures for School Television in Great Cities, 1966-67	33
G.	Expenditures for School Television — 1966-67	35
H.	Number of Interviews Using Questionnaires	64

GLOSSARY

CCTV — **Closed Circuit Television.** The system used to distribute a television signal (both audio and video) from the point of origin to the point of display by means of cables.

CATV — **Community Antenna System.** A re-distribution system using a common antenna, generally of high sensitivity, to intercept a television broadcast signal for relay via CCTV to a number of display points.

ETV — **Educational Television.** A generic term applied to non-commercial television operations. Instructional Television, Public Television, and School Television may be considered forms of ETV.

ITV — **Instructional Television.** Television programming aimed at the student, either in the classroom or otherwise, in the general context of curriculum oriented formal education.

ITFS — **Instructional Television Fixed Service.** The 31 television channels set aside by the Federal Communications Commission in the 2500-2690 megacycle band for use by educational institutions and organizations for transmission of instructional, cultural, and other types of educationally related materials. Translators are necessary at place of reception or origin of CCTV system.

MPATI — **Midwest Program on Airborne Television Instruction.** An experimental airborne instructional television system which uses an aircraft flying at 25-30,000 feet as the transmitting site. MPATI broadcasts to schools within a six state area from a point in east central Indiana.

PTV — **Public Television.** That television programming of human interest and importance which is not available nor appropriate for support by advertising and which is neither devised for formal education nor as a means of communication by school systems.

STV — **School Television.** Television programming pertinent to the operation and mission of school systems. Included are the uses of TV for direct instruction, school administrative purposes, teacher in-service education, and community information and education.

Translator — An electronic device capable of picking up a TV signal from one source of transmission or channel and re-transmitting it on another channel.

UHF — **Ultra High Frequency.** For TV, the UHF frequency band extends from 470-890 megacycles for channels 14-83.

VHF — **Very High Frequency.** For TV, the VHF frequency band extends from 44-88 megacycles for channels 2-6 and from 174-216 megacycles for channels 7-13.

VTR — **Video Tape Recorder/Recording.** The Recorder is an electronic device capable of recording the audio and video signals from a TV system on a special magnetic tape which can be re-played immediately or stored for a later playback. The Recording is the magnetic tape so recorded.

2500 megacycle/megahertz. An alternate designation for ITFS. Megacycle (Mc/s) and megahertz (MHz) are synonymous and may be used interchangeably.

INTRODUCTION

My full-time work as head of the Research Council staff began in January, 1968, after this study had been completed and circulated. My first reaction was one of appreciation for its well-marshaled information and conviction that its findings can be extremely useful.

I feel strongly that for the sake of quality education in large city public schools, the Research Council should exert every effort to put the recommendations of this study into action at the earliest possible dates.

Fortunately, the Instructional Materials Committee met in Boston in May, 1968, and formulated the recommendations that follow. The Research Council ratified these one day later. They officially provide us with a "hunting license," authorizing those activities for which financing can be obtained.

The uncertainties that attend Congressional appropriations for fiscal 1969 have seriously delayed the carrying forward of cooperative action on school television in the Great Cities. The potentials of television for strengthened instruction, for improved administrative communication, for more effective in-service teacher education, and for public education are too important to be permitted to remain dormant.

It is my fervent hope that every decision-making officer of federal, state, and private funding agencies will read this study carefully and will assist the Research Council of the Great Cities to implement the recommendations here.

Alva Dittrick, Executive Vice President
Research Council of the Great Cities
Program for School Improvement

Television in Urban Education

MOST ACUTE INSTRUCTIONAL PROBLEMS
(BY CITIES)

	CURRICULUM	TEACHERS	ENVIRONMENT	WORKLOAD	COMMUNICATION	ADMINISTRATION	FINANCES	FACILITIES	
Baltimore	10	9	6	3	2	3	2	1	36
Boston	4	5	6	3	1	2	—	—	21
Buffalo	6	8	3	—	1	1	4	1	24
Chicago	3	6	6	4	1	1	1	—	22
Cleveland	8	13	13	7	6	2	—	—	45
Detroit	9	7	2	2	—	1	—	1	22
Los Angeles	16	14	8	6	8	3	4	—	54
Memphis	2	7	7	5	1	—	1	2	24
Milwaukee	7	10	6	6	1	2	2	2	36
New York	13	11	10	1	3	1	—	—	39
Philadelphia	11	9	2	1	4	2	—	—	30
Pittsburgh	11	14	6	4	5	4	1	2	47
San Diego	12	6	5	3	2	3	2	1	34
San Francisco	12	6	9	2	4	3	1	3	40
St. Louis	12	13	10	4	1	—	2	3	50
Wash. D.C.	6	3	—	—	2	2	1	—	14
No. of Responses	142	141	94	56	41	30	22	17	543

▥ Most frequently mentioned acute problem
☰ 2nd most frequently mentioned acute problem
▨ 3rd "   "   "   "   "   "   "   "

An average of 2.5 problems were mentioned in each of the 218 interviews

Figure 2

THE MOST ACUTE INSTRUCTIONAL PROBLEMS

AS SEEN BY PERSONS WITH DIFFERENT PROFESSIONAL RESPONSIBILITIES

AREAS OF CONCERN	PROFESSIONAL GROUPS: Superintendents & Board Members	Administrators	Supervisors	Principals	Teachers	Inst. Material & TV Personnel	
Curriculum	14	55	26	16	16	14	142
Teachers	9	39	34	22	24	13	141
Environment	4	27	21	15	21	6	94
Workload	1	2	14	15	23	1	56
Communication	2	12	12	4	9	2	41
Administration	—	7	2	5	9	7	30
Finances	4	7	4	2	1	4	21
Facilities	1	4	4	4	4	—	17
No. of Responses out of 218 Interviews	35	153	117	83	107	47	*543*

Most frequently mentioned acute problem
2nd most frequently mentioned acute problem
3rd " " " " " " " " " "

Figure 3

(d) **Excessive teacher load** covers too many pupils per teacher, not enough time to prepare lessons—amid new curriculum demands—or to give individual attention, too many non-teaching duties, too few teacher aides or insufficient specialized help, and—sometimes when specialists are available—too many interruptions in the school day.

(e) **Poor communication** among administrators, teachers, parents, children, and their communities encompasses teachers' ignorance of school policies and of their pupils' home and neighborhood conditions, their inability to fathom what the children care about, the students' incomprehension of how schooling can affect their lives, parents' lack of involvement in their children's education, and the relative inability of school systems to obtain help from city-wide and neighborhood leaders for marshalling more and better resources that could advance effective schooling.

(f) **Administrative leadership and practices** unequal to the schools' tasks include the plethora of red tape necessary to get anything done, unclear and even conflicting policies, inconsistent practices, and failure to distribute existing resource materials when and where the teachers need them.

(g) **Insufficient and/or unpredictable financial support** is congruent with low budgets, unsatisfactory policies governing federal and some foundation aid programs, meagerness of State aid to city schools, absence of school board control over local taxes, and the eroded tax base in major cities.

(h) **Inadequate facilities** are too little work and storage space; its poor arrangement for changed uses and new technical resources; insufficient, fragile, and incompetently purchased equipment; and poor maintenance.

Of 466 school people we interviewed, 393 gave their opinions on the most acute problems. Most mentioned more than one problem, some four or more. We tabulated 543 responses.

More **persons** brought up curricular factors than any other set of problems. And the highest number of **responses** dealt with needs for greater teacher quality and quantity. Environmental realities such as language deficiencies, experiential and physical deprivation, low motivation and high mobility of pupils and their families were the third largest group of replies, followed by (4th) excessive teacher loads, (5th) poor communication, (6th) defects in administrative leadership and practices, (7th) insufficient or unpredictable financial support, and (8th) inadequate facilities.

Eight cities—Baltimore, Detroit, Los Angeles, New York, Philadelphia, San Diego, San Francisco, and Washington, D.C.—gave most responses to curriculum problems. Three—Buffalo, Milwaukee, and Pittsburgh—put teacher weaknesses and shortages first, while three others (Chicago, Cleveland, and Memphis) gave teacher deficiencies and adverse environmental conditions equally high priority. Boston put most stress on externally imposed conditions. St. Louis was the only city which gave excessive teacher workload greatest weight. (See Appendix C for a further detailed breakdown of responses.)

II. SCHOOL TELEVISION IN THE GREAT CITIES

This section digests combined findings on the status of television in the 16 public school systems. Appendix D supplies brief accounts of the separate **School Television** organizational patterns, programs, their reported use, and TV facilities in each city.

1. **Programs and Uses**

Functions of television. In 1966-67, about nine-tenths of more than 5,300 hours of school telecasts, not counting repeat programs, were devoted to "direct instruction." These were programs intended primarily for **viewing by students**. About one out of 17 hours was used for **in-service education**, designed to be viewed by teachers. Slightly less than one in 34 hours was for **community information** and **education**, including at-home adult courses. Less than one of every 79 hours was used for **administrative communication**.

A large part of telecast "direct instruction" is considered to be curriculum enrichment: optional supplements to the substance the classroom teacher presents.

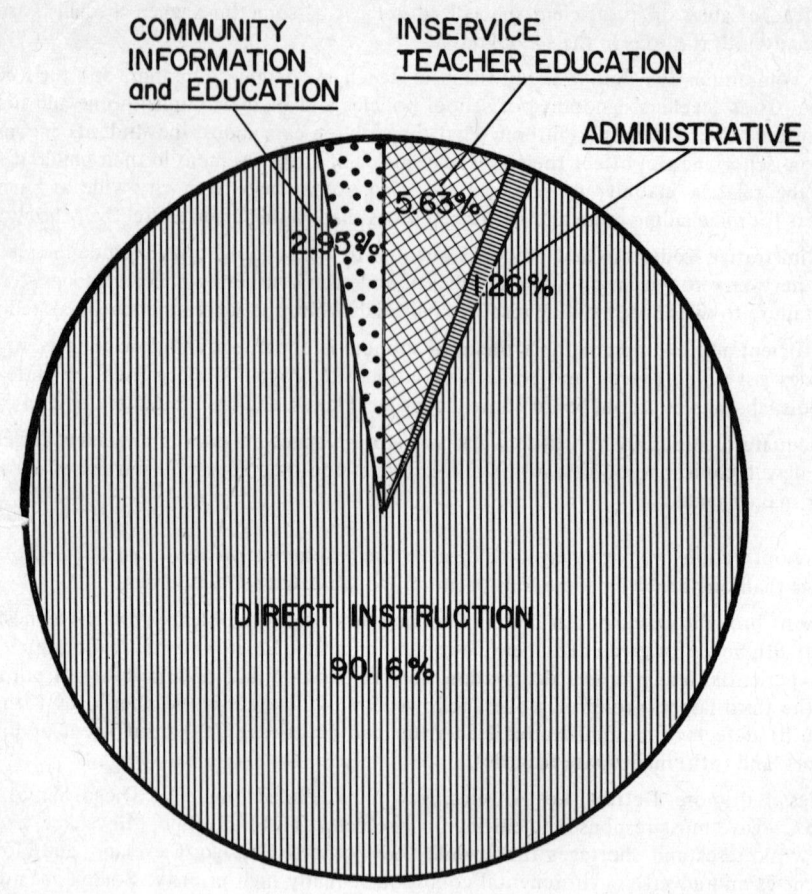

SCHOOL TELEVISION USES

Great Cities — 1966-'67

BASE: 100% equals 5,311 hours of school TV transmission, excluding repeat programs

SOURCES: The Individual City Public School Systems

Figure 4

TABLE A

PERCENTAGE OF TOTAL SCHOOL HOURS
FOR WHICH INSTRUCTIONAL TELEVISION IS AVAILABLE
(K-12)

Assuming that there are 180 days in an average school year and that approximately five hours per day are devoted to instruction, each grade has a possible 900 hours of schooling per year. Considering all grades (K-12), this would give a total of 11,700 hours of school time that must be filled with some type of learning experience. On this basis, the average number of original (excluding repeats) broadcast television instructional hours for all of the Great Cities is 320 per school year. Thus ITV is seen to provide less than 3% of the total possible hours of classroom instruction for the Great Cities. The city-by-city breakdown based on this assumption is:

City	Percentage
Baltimore	.67%
Boston	1.19
Buffalo	1.94
Chicago	3.03
Cleveland	2.26
Detroit	10.00
Los Angeles	1.83
Memphis	3.08
Milwaukee	1.83
New York	2.02
Philadelphia	4.29
Pittsburgh	2.34
San Diego*	2.31
San Francisco	2.41
St. Louis	2.86
Washington, D. C.	---
AVERAGE (excluding Washington)	2.80

* Telecasts began in February, 1967

PERCENTAGE OF ELEMENTARY & SECONDARY ENROLLMENTS REPORTED AS REGULAR USERS OF ITV

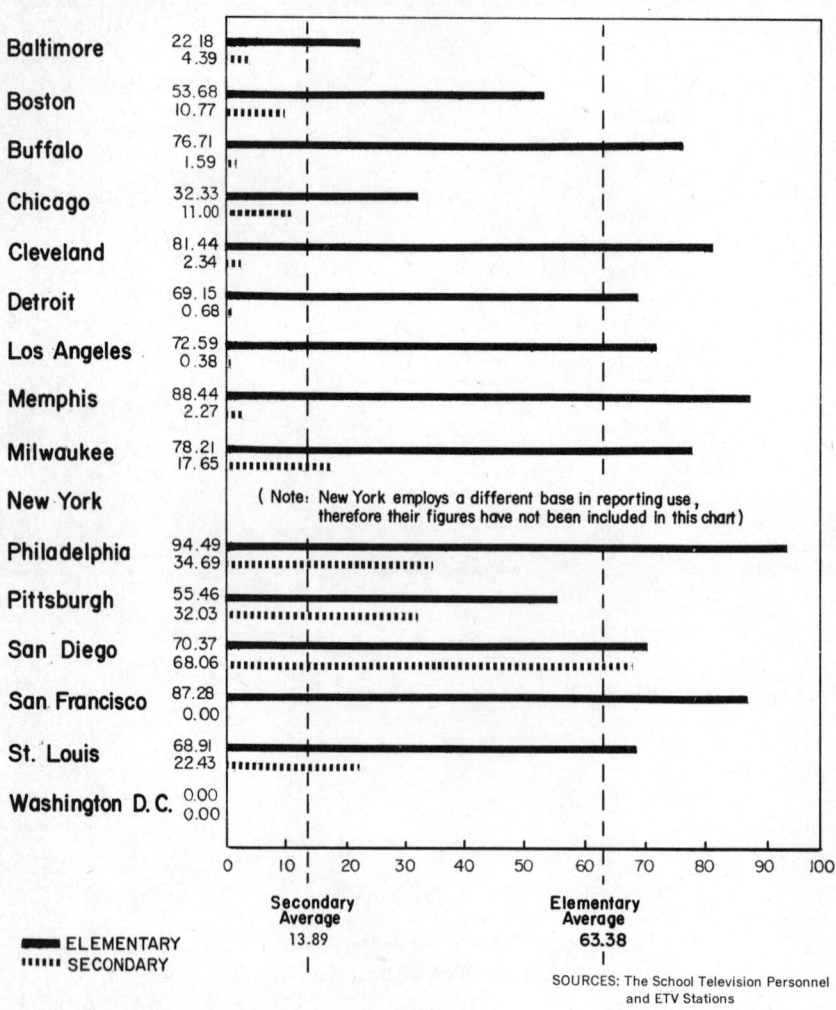

Figure 5

TABLE B

INTERVIEWEES' AVERAGE "GUESSTIMATES" OF "REGULAR USERS" OF ITV*

CITY	ELEMENTARY	SECONDARY
Baltimore	57%	13%
Boston	18	16
Buffalo	55	25
Chicago	14	20
Cleveland	31	7
Detroit	29	2
Los Angeles	43	2
Memphis	95	1
Milwaukee	64	6
New York	80	1
Philadelphia	60	17
Pittsburgh	59	14
San Diego	34	3
San Francisco	63	5
St. Louis	21	3
Washington, D. C.	--	--

100% equals enrolled students
* Regular user was defined as using ITV on an average of at least once per week.

The words **enrichment** and **supplementary** have different meanings from city to city. Memphis school people say their programs are all supplementary, but teachers there appear to rely upon televised Science, Music, and Art lessons for core content of those subjects in their classrooms. Pittsburgh appears to have done most to identify for teachers which school series are entirely sequential in their presentation of content, which series are not, and which ones have certain groupings of lessons that are considered essential and should be viewed sequentially, while other parts of the series are optional.

Amount of programming. There are wide differences in the hours of **school television** transmission, excluding repeat programs, among the cities.* In 1966-67 Detroit transmitted 1,255 hours (over 9,000 hours if we include repeat programs) over five channels: the community-owned WTVS under the Detroit ETV Foundation, two translators using taped Midwest Program for Airborne Televised Instruction (MPATI) Series, and two 2,500 megacycle channels owned by Detroit Public Schools. Washington had no officially approved use of **school television** in 1966-67, because of disappointing trials in 1960. There were reports of covert tuning by some District of Columbia teachers to programs telecast by the Greater Washington ETV Association. In the fall of 1967 three Washington schools—one in a middle-income area, one from low-income high-rise apartments, and a third from disadvantaged homes—began using WETA, Channel 26, telecasts with a TV set in every classroom.

Amount of use. Data from all sources indicate that large numbers of pupils view **School TV** in the Great Cities. Two qualifications are necessary. First, the share of regular users compared with total enrollment varies tremendously from city to city. Teachers who use programs regularly employ television from 15 minutes (minimum) to one hour 20 minutes (maximum) per week. Some "regular users" tend to use fewer lessons in a series as the year goes on. Second, the evaluation methods used by ETV stations and school departments to give an accurate accounting of use—largely consisting of questionnaires voluntarily answered by teachers and the quantities of teachers' guides requested—are inexact, unreliable, and coarse. These statistics result from collection of data, however incomplete. They are more accurate than guesstimates of system-wide use made by administrators and teachers. We asked for guesses and got them. All they prove is that hardly any of the people we interviewed know what use of television in their school system had been reported—or that they do not believe the reports.

Grade levels. Two-thirds of Great Cities' **School TV** programming in 1966-67 was intended for elementary grades. The almost universally volunteered reason is that secondary school schedules forbid use of TV for all but a small fraction of students. Considering this firmly-held belief, a surprisingly large part of the Great City **school TV** transmission—one-fifth—was directed to junior high schools. That was just about the national average. High school programming in the Great Cities, on the other hand, was only half as much as in the U.S. as a whole.

Elementary teachers, we were repeatedly told, seem to feel less threatened by having team-teaching partners (in person and on television) who know more than they do in some subjects, are less confident of their abilities to teach "hard" subjects like Science and Mathematics, and are more hospitable to innovation than secondary teachers. They also have more flexibility in deciding how to allocate hours in their school day and week.

Largest 1966-67 transmission hours were directed to intermediate grades 4-6. The peak was at grade 6. Reports from teachers showed definite divergences from intended grade levels. Some city teachers tuned to programs designed for younger, and (less often) older grades, especially in Reading and Math.

There is twice as much programming for primary grade children in Great Cities as in the nation at large. This may reflect increasing concern for teaching inner-city children during their early, formative years. The teaching of Phonics for Reading gets intensive, careful attention in Buffalo, Detroit, and other cities' primary **school TV** series.

Subject distribution. Science, Foreign Languages, Social Studies, English and Language Arts, and the Arts (including Music) received most televised hours, in that order. The first two are subjects in which elementary teachers are said to feel they need the most help, or where elementary teachers' knowledge is

---

*The quantity of repeat transmission is not well defined from city to city; statistical compilations in this Study omit them.

SCHOOL TELEVISION PROGRAMMING IN THE GREAT CITIES, 1966-'67 COMPARED WITH NATIONAL DATA FOR ONE WEEK IN APRIL, 1966
(By Grade Levels)

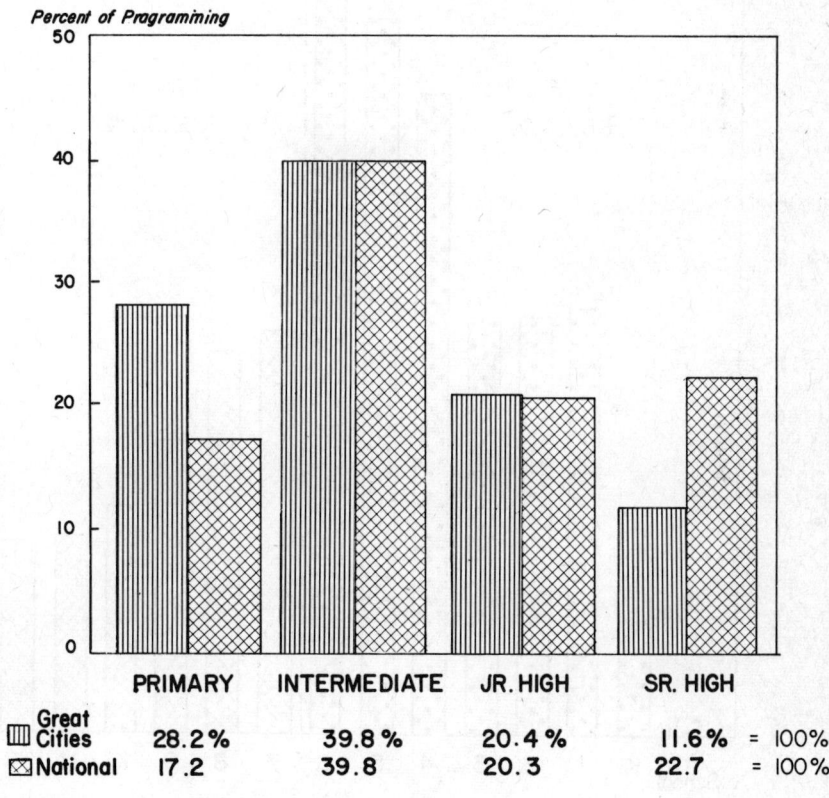

Figure 6

SCHOOL TELEVISION BROADCAST PROGRAMMING BY GRADE LEVEL
Great Cities, 1966-'67

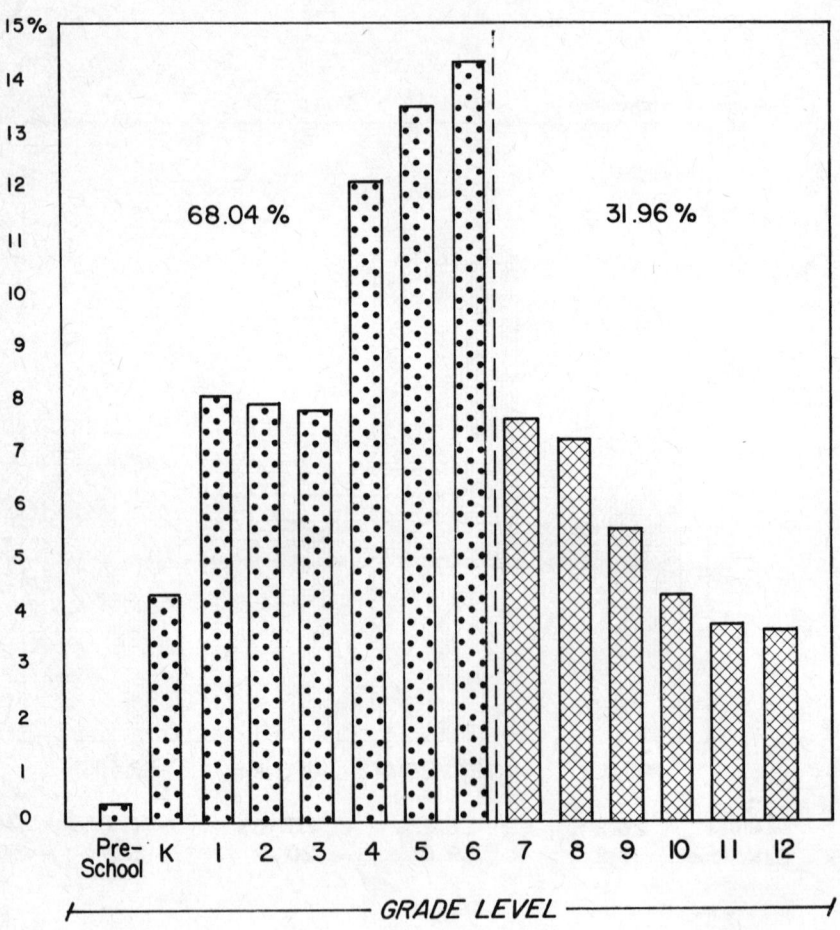

SOURCES: The Individual City Public School Systems and ETV Stations

Figure 7

GREAT CITIES SCHOOL TELEVISION PROGRAM SOURCES

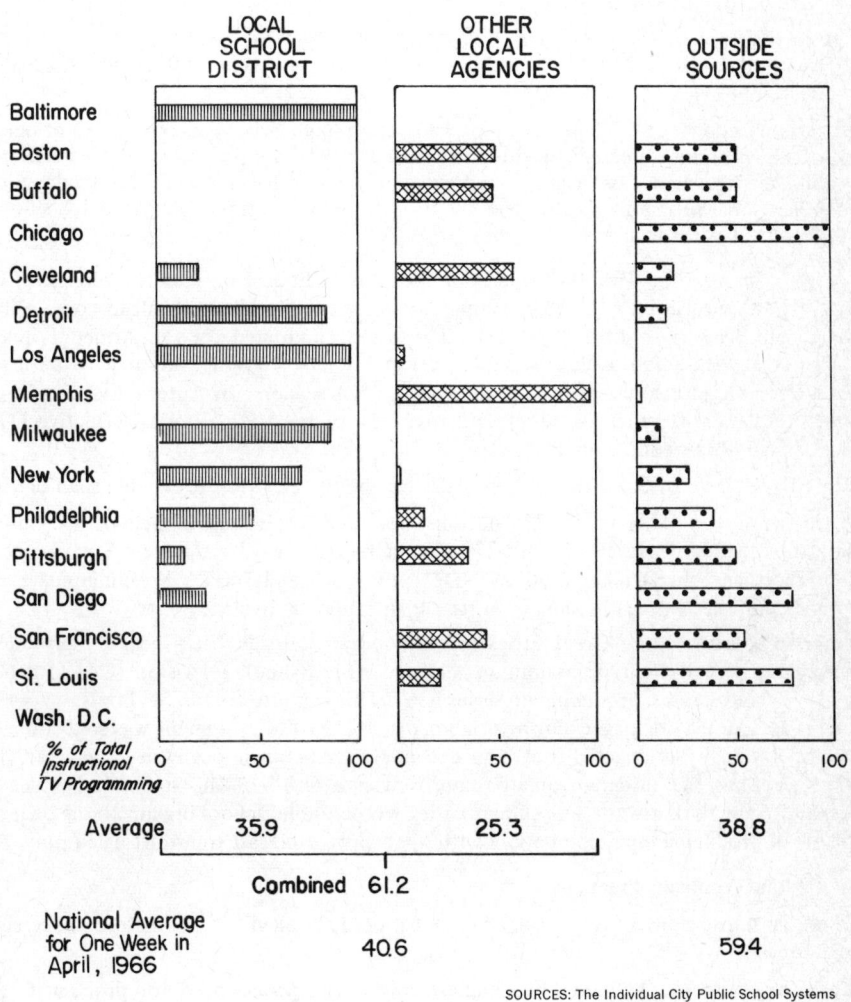

Figure 9

least satisfactory to their supervisors. People told us that because of the poor content knowledge of many teachers and their college preparation, it may be that television helped to make possible the introduction of some new courses which might otherwise have been impossible.

Before kindergarten? We found sharp differences in opinion whether television is beneficial for disadvantaged pre-school children. Both the Director of Early Childhood Education in New York and the Senior Consultant to Head Start programs at the Office of Economic Opportunity in Washington asserted that these children need, more than anything else, first-hand experience with friendly adults and a wide range of experiences touching and manipulating objects. There is, however, great need for the in-service training of pre-school teachers and teacher aides working with inner-city youngsters. Television, they said, should be used for orientation of these instructors.

Cleveland has a PROGRAM FOR PARENTS series viewed by groups of mothers at each of its 68 Child Development (Head Start) Centers. Los Angeles was producing a television series for parents of pre-school children in the summer of 1967.

Vocational education? Much of junior and senior high **school television** is enrichment of **academic** instruction. Exceptions directed to students' future employability were New York's and Philadelphia's series, and Detroit's and Los Angeles' individual programs for teachers on Guidance and Counseling, Detroit's occasional programs on Business and Vocational Education, and Pittsburgh's non-credit 90 lesson series on Electronics for teachers.

As with the pre-schoolers, the experts on Vocational Education disagree whether TV is useful. Some are certain that acquisition of motor, manipulative, and kinesthetic skills can come only by doing, with individual help. This is contrary to results of research conducted for the Armed Forces. The Parks Job Corps Center at Pleasanton, California, outside San Francisco, also reports that its most effective televised programs were on Electronics Test Equipment, tutorial sessions on Automotive Gas Engines, Counseling and Job Interview self-evaluation tapes, and that—except for Math—its least effective ITV experience has been with general basic education.

The City College of San Francisco uses closed circuit television for a wide span of vocational courses.

Commercial and Educational TV stations are somewhat ahead of **School TV** units in attempts to serve vocational students. In 1967 WOR-TV, Channel 11, owned by the New York **Daily News**, telecast a series on Shorthand. In October, 1967 WNDT New York and WETA Washington began transmitting a series whose purpose is to enable adults to pass high school equivalency tests.

Program sources. Many Great Cities rely on sources outside their local TV production facilities for substantial portions of their programming. Chicago Area School Television (CAST) depends 100% upon imports for school service, producing no series itself. This was also true in St. Louis, whose ETV station had its cameras so seriously damaged during a labor dispute that its equipment was sold for spare parts. Forced to rely upon nationally syndicated programs, except for series taped locally in prior years, there were candid St. Louis reactions that program quality improved as a result of this impasse. Detroit, Milwaukee, Los Angeles, and New York are the only Great Cities whose public school organizations own production facilities capable of producing tapes compatible with open circuit telecast transmitting equipment.

2. **Some Promising Practices**

There is strong consensus in many Great Cities that television has helped make significant gains in particular areas.

Local involvement. We found the highest enthusiasm pronounced for program fare which does not pretend to have professional production qualities: the closed circuit telecasts in and from the Byrd School in Chicago to a cluster of five schools (a network being replicated in four new clusters in 1967-68); with the exception of a full-time TV teacher for Science, all other lessons were presented on TV by regular classroom teachers. In Buffalo, even an unwisely designed closed circuit system enabled teachers without television training to present 15-minute close-up segments of sewing operations difficult to show to large classes; speech teachers there employed a videotape recorder for children to see their progress in overcoming speech defects. At the Conwell and other "magnet schools" in Philadelphia, paid non-professional housewives supervise reportedly successful closed circuit programming.

TV quality vs. school function. Satisfaction of teachers and principals with **School TV** appears mainly to grow from process, as in Memphis, Chicago, Detroit, San Diego, and elsewhere, when curriculum supervisors, content specialists, and classroom teachers work together to revise what the courses teach. It is quite possible that in these situations TV **serves mainly as a catalyst for change**, always hard to bring about, and that other means could conceivably serve as well.

In summarizing his observations of school TV and radio in developing countries, Wilbur Schramm concluded that where these media were used to meet requirements for which other resources were unavailable, they were successful. Where countries had the facilities, but felt no overriding needs for their use, the results were indifferent or temporary. Milwaukee's Health and Physical Education people regard the Crest dental hygiene program—telecast while students used tablets showing bacilli in their mouths—as successful; the number of hours for hygienists to demonstrate the same lesson in classrooms was larger than available personnel could possibly provide.

Many administrators and teachers castigated the quality of **School TV** programs. From any central source, they appear to expect professionally polished production, even though they often do not get it from commercial and educational stations, much less school-wrought telecasts. When they and their colleagues are involved in planning, and more so when they take part in carrying out plans, their critical attitude virtually evaporates. They seem to be much more concerned with specific lesson content and methods when they have a choice in selection of outside series and something to say about preparations for and use of home-made series.

Introducing new curricula. Everett Chaffee of Los Angeles told how television helped orient their elementary teachers in new Science curricula. First, supervisors from the eight districts met with the author of the new state-adopted text. These eight people then conducted workshops in their districts, bringing in one person from each elementary school. That person led discussion after a televised series beamed to teachers in his school, aided by supportive printed materials. In essence, TV provided a floor of basic communication which Dr. Chaffee said, "brings it all together."

Detroit people spoke of their using television as "the cutting edge of the curriculum." In addition to using TV to introduce new concepts in Mathematics to teachers, at the request of the Parents' associations Detroit produced a series titled NEW MATH FOR PARENTS.

Access to more visual material. New York's program production quality is as polished as any. Even with the Board of Education's new production center and experienced staff, there is constant need to identify and obtain the right pictorial materials. Several corporate and instructional media people in New York have formed the Metropolitan Area Council for Instructional Television Resources (MACITVR). Its aim is to effect cooperation between commercial and educational organizations. One project, they hope will be underwritten by the New York Board of Trade, is a computerized register of film footage.

Improving teacher competence. One of the potentially most important new advances is Micro-teaching. This use of videotape enables a teacher to see, study, and improve upon the effects he has on students. Developed by Dwight Allen and his group at Stanford, television serves here as a retroactive mirror. In at least three large metropolitan areas there are interesting variants: as part of Baltimore Public Schools' Project Mission, in cooperation with local colleges, to prepare teachers for work in inner-city schools; at San Francisco State College (with help from Robert Bell of Rutgers), for sensitivity training of Upward Bound project personnel; at San Francisco City College for general pre-service teacher training; and at Manhattan College, New York, where—among other gains—there are indications that Micro-teaching may aid in determining temperamental fitness for a teaching career.

One primary difficulty, we were told, is that even the most extensive in-service programs of teacher education require thorough review. Teachers often regard them as irksome rather than of any use for doing their work. We noted very strong enthusiasms expressed by Directors of English, Math, Social Studies, Science, and Foreign Languages for televised courses, combining small group discussions with teachers. Few said that any in-service programs were relevant to the most acute needs in 1966-67. When we viewed what some of the most earnest people had helped produce that year, we saw that in-service teacher education has a long way to go.

Other difficulties are limits upon required after-school time in teacher contracts, the rising conviction that extra work deserves extra pay, and the strong preference for taking those courses which apply toward the next salary column and yield academic credits. Teachers regarded being able to view courses from their own schools or homes an important plus.

One Science series televised for New York elementary teachers was considered successful. 2,000 teachers registered and completed the course without credit. A classroom teacher named Mary demonstrated the experiments on camera. She made no bones about being strictly a non-scientist. Mary made mistakes, then cheerfully and un-selfconsciously corrected them. According to Dr. Schenberg, New York's Supervisor of Science, the participating teacher's reaction was typically, "Well, if Mary can teach that, so can I."

Need breeds invention. San Diego has two recent examples of need spurring creative uses of **school TV**. When the threat of LSD aroused the community, a still-new ITV production organization produced a program in three days. It showed students asking authoritative psychiatric consultants about the effects of this drug.

When there was demand for televised instruction at the secondary level, with the same scheduling problems which are considered insuperable barriers in many other places, San Diego transmitted programs picked up by a videotape recorder at Morse High School. Debugging with antenna adjustments was needed for a sharp picture. When a two-year program for videotape recorders has been carried out, it will be possible for San Diego to transmit secondary programs for off-air taping, so that each school can replay tapes as its schedule dictates.

Teaching adults. One practice not new, but receiving increasingly purposeful work, is the exploitation of television's adult education potentials.

Chicago's TV College, with its correspondence courses over WTTW-TV to at-home students for credit as part of the city's free junior college program, is now in its 11th year. Los Angeles adult course offerings show a sharp upward curve in registrations, led by **Escuela** which teaches English as a Second Language. Philadelphia's Operation Alphabet began in 1961 over WFIL-TV with sponsorship of the Junior Chamber, the Council of Churches, Philadelphia Foundation, and 41 other civic, business, labor, and service organizations. It received 100 half-hour tapes from the Minnesota Mining & Manufacturing Company for the National Association of Public School Adult Educators to carry forward a national effort against functional illiteracy. Baltimore's LEARNING TO READ has a reported enrollment of 6,000 adults.

In September, 1967 five ETV stations joined with the State and City universities of New York to offer six college courses as the University of the Air. Viewers who pay tuition fees take final examinations on campus at 11 colleges.

Administrative uses of television are in their infancy. Several Great City Superintendents—among them Drs. Crowther of Los Angeles, Donovan of New York, Kottmeyer of St. Louis, Marland of Pittsburgh, Stimbert of Memphis and Dailard of San Diego—have been demonstrating the value of televised communication with their staffs, parents, and the general public. Commercial stations cooperate with coverage.

New York's program explaining retirement system changes to teachers had an estimated audience of 54,000. Cleveland gave televised directions to all its teachers for preparation of the State personnel report. Milwaukee's nine SCHOOL BOARD REPORTS programs had an estimated 25,000 viewers. Memphis schedules ten Faculty Meetings of the Air. Philadelphia's regional meetings for parents had estimated armchair attendance of 10,000.

In New York 500 to 700 questions are telephoned in during each monthly telecast for the Superintendent to answer. Volunteers from parent organizations man telephones at commercial station WABC, which pays all production costs including film sequences made in schools. Since limited time forbids telecast replies to every question, Dr. Donovan's office answers all others by mail.

For several years, Baltimore's commercial station WBAL-TV has aired the Superintendent's annual staff meeting in September. A Buffalo program on racial integration for all administrators and teachers had estimated attendance of 3,300. Chicago had a police officer talk to children about summer safety; televised an Achievement Assembly presenting awards to students who excelled in After School programs, and a series of Parent Council meetings featuring Negro Heritage telecasts.

Pittsburgh is the only city we encountered whose Superintendent had an audience analysis made, to learn how many persons viewed his televised report, how many had heard of it, and how many could identify him.

In nearly every Great City, school personnel we interviewed praised television consistently for such communication. Many remarked there should be much more of it.

3. Facilities and Operations

School Television facilities include open circuit broadcast, closed circuit, and Instructional Television Fixed Services (ITFS) over 2500 megacycles.

Patterns of Ownership and Control

Only New York City's Board of Education owns its own TV broadcast channel, having earlier been a participant in and major underwriter of **School Television** Service through the Educational Broadcasting Corporation which operates WNDT, Channel 13. New York City schools have received help too, from the city's municipal station, WNYC-TV which operates UHF Channel 31. WNYC-TV has a staff of 50 and $600,000 budget, and provides in-service instruction for police, firemen, public health nurses, and other large, scattered groups of civil service personnel. The city public schools also operate eight CCTV systems.

One city has evolved, using a traditional instrument for new opportunities, a hybrid school-controlled ETV station. The autonomous Milwaukee Board of Vocational and Adult Education, whose origins go back to 1912, owns two channels. The Board, created by State statute like others across Wisconsin, has taxing powers. Its members are elected by the Milwaukee Board of School Directors. The public school system appears presently content with transmission over one of the TV channels.

These two were the only Great Cities' school-owned open circuit television channels in 1966-67. All the others (except Washington) work through the larger metropolitan commercial and educational TV stations, with widely differing relationships.

San Diego has invented a new organizational device, an area Instructional Television Authority based on a contract among participating school systems. Wholly concerned with instruction, it buys studio facilities and time from the ETV station centered at San Diego State College.

Most Great Cities' school systems share in area public or ETV station operations, usually contributing a substantial part toward these stations' daytime costs. Others pay for some commercial station time in combination with time contributed as a public service. A few do both.

Production help from the commercial stations, as in Baltimore and Philadelphia, is considered good. But times of day available are not enough, nor best for the schools.

In Boston, cordial civilities are exchanged between officers of the Public Schools and WGBH's regional **21 Inch Classroom**. The Boston schools appear to get little of direct relevance to their instructional problems for $42,000 annual payment. The city's attitude is that the programs may be right for suburban Newton and Lexington, but are of little use for students in Roxbury or South Boston.

Such conflicts of interest between ETV and Great City schools are common. St. Louis Public Schools paid $100,000 toward the $350,000 total 1966-67 budget of KETC, Channel 9. If city schools withdrew their support, this ETV station would be in serious financial trouble, even though it has obtained about $50,000 in increased memberships from other school systems.

Los Angeles Unified School District has received funding authorization to acquire UHF Channel 58. Superintendent Crowther has estimated this would double present school use of TV, while saving $150,000 now annually used to buy TV time from ETV and commercial stations. This would mean a loss to Community Television of Southern California, Inc., which operates KCET, owns Channel 28, and needs every dollar it can find.

The school programs of Community ETV stations from East to West tend to serve the suburbs' curricular preferences. Their leadership and financial contributions are primarily suburban, but city money helps keep them shakily alive.

TABLE D

OWNERSHIP OF TV CHANNELS USED BY GREAT CITIES' SCHOOLS
1966-67

CITY	SCHOOL UHF	SCHOOL 2500 MHz	COMMUNITY VHF	COMMUNITY UHF	COMMERCIAL VHF	COMMERCIAL UHF	TOTAL
Baltimore					3		3
Boston			1	1			2
Buffalo				1	1		2
Chicago			1	1			2
Cleveland				1	1		2
Detroit		2+2*		1			5
Los Angeles				1	3	1	5
Memphis			1				1
Milwaukee			1	1			2
New York	1				1		2
Philadelphia			1	1	1		3
Pittsburgh			1	1	3		5
St. Louis			1		3		4
San Diego				1			1
San Francisco			1				1
Washington, D. C.				1**			

*Two of these are 2500Mc and two translator channels are used to re-transmit MPATI programs.

**ETV channel available in the area, but was not used by the Washington, D. C. Public Schools.

Harmonious relationships evidently exist between city schools and public ETV stations in Cleveland, Memphis, Pittsburgh, and San Diego. Cleveland and San Diego have new ETV stations whose organization owes much to the school Superintendents' initiative. Cleveland's WVIZ used Max S. Hayes Vocational School as headquarters its first two years. These schools and stations are in their honeymoon phase. All four of these cities have station people who seem to be proving that they are more interested in schools than are many ETV personnel. Educators in all these places anticipate that if the schools are to serve more of city children's needs, eventual television requirements will far exceed the capacity of their area's open circuit broadcast channels.

Two alternatives to a sole dependence upon open circuit community broadcasting are exemplified by Detroit's use of 2,500-megacycle channels and Chicago's closed circuit clusters.

Detroit, with five channels, has a diverse mix: There are two 2,500-megacycle bands; it holds a $200,000 annual membership in MPATI and pays $60,000 to $70,000 a year to the Detroit ETV Foundation, which owns Channel 56 and transmits programs produced in large part by Detroit Public Schools. An estimated 200 other school systems use these programs, for which Detroit receives no financial credit. The two 2,500-megacycle bands, which went on the air in November, 1965, will be expanded to four channels in the near future.

Chicago is a member of Chicago Area School Television (CAST) to which it pays $85,000 per year, but its most effective use of TV is reportedly in closed circuit clusters.

Personnel

Media Supervisors. Most **School TV** people are versatile. They have to be. The trend is for broadcasting units to come under a **Directorship of Instructional Materials**, now filled in Philadelphia and Milwaukee by the persons who had been directly in charge of **school TV**. Baltimore is considering reorganization, which may eventually establish an Assistant Superintendent for Educational Media.

The instructional materials officer usually reports to an Assistant Superintendent for Curriculum and/or Instruction. The Director of **School TV** ordinarily has only fleeting contact with the Superintendent. Directors of Instructional Materials whose backgrounds are primarily in the Library and Audio-visual fields are not always proponents of **School Television**. Some believe, understandably, that other options pay off with greater learning results. **School TV** people are another competing force with their own particular vision. Few media people work together toward achieving defined instructional goals.

In at least six Great Cities the **Directors of School TV** are veterans of educational radio. The new (1965) Cleveland ETV station and San Diego ITV Authority (1967) have employed as key executive officers men who earned recognition as school telecasters. Although any generalization based on sex is fraught with hazard, one of our principal investigators observed that women in **school TV** were trying more innovative approaches than were the men, who were more often concerned with finished qualities of production. Of course, we also met excellent men who are breaking new ground.

Qualifications are generally postgraduate degrees, demonstrable experience but not necessarily formal training in TV management and production, and teaching experience in secondary or higher education. Personal qualities which six effective Directors of **School Television** have in common are enthusiasm, energy and unflappability in crises. Budgeteering and grantsmanship help. Job conditions require resourcefulness amid too much to do, too little budget, insufficient staff, materials, equipment, and time for the work load.

A different category of persons are **ETV station officials** responsible for school services. Four of them we met evinced serious interest in city schools' acute problems. Two supervise operations apparently satisfactory to Superintendents. Two are too new on their jobs to predict if this will be so. From all signs we saw, the work of the five others is highly regarded by their Station Managers, Boards, or Commissions. Their services to suburban classrooms are adequate or better. If they are aware of the extent of City schools' dissatisfaction with what is being telecast, they have more pressing problems elsewhere.

In 1966-67 two Great Cities had nobody actually in charge of what their schools wanted and got from EVT stations. With rare exceptions ETV producer-directors were providing quick, cursory advice to TV teachers.

Television teachers. They are specialists who must be generalists: working with curriculum specialists and teacher-supervisor committees on planning; doing research; writing scripts and teachers' guides; gathering visual materials and properties, and presenting their lessons with minimal rehearsal before going on camera.

Less burdened situations deserve attention. One Milwaukee art teacher, Kent Anderson, teaches every lesson to a class before he televises it and usually makes a live TV presentation before taping. Detroit's classroom teachers know that the first semester of each series is a trial run. Feedback is candid. After a gaffe, the TV teacher will hear "Boy, did you goof today!" New York allots a TV teacher about one week for planning and two hours stage time for set-up, rehearsal, and taping a 20-minute lesson. Buffalo takes five hours for a 30-minute taping.

Most TV teachers are recruited after having shown classroom skills and mastery of their subject areas, and are chosen on the basis of a taped "sample" lesson they have prepared. They seldom receive formal training in TV elements, although some cities provide summer workshop orientation. Most learn by doing. In two cities they do not become permanent TV teachers until after a full year's work on camera. Philadelphia requires a Master's degree and written examination. Of the 179 full- and part-time TV teachers reported on Great Cities payrolls or on loan to ETV stations, some have had considerable experience. Examples abound. Mary Ellen Rohun and Ethel Convel teach A POCKETFUL OF FUN for pre-schoolers, having broadcast nine and eight years respectively in New York. Shirley Brown has been doing LET'S TELL A STORY for three elementary levels over eight years, and Mrs. Naomi Bauernfeind has telecast LEARNING TO READ at two adult levels for seven years in Baltimore.

Six Great City systems pay TV teachers no salary differential above their regular salaries. Three have no such specialists. Six systems provide for additional pay. These increments are $66 per month in Los Angeles, 10% of regular teaching salary in Pittsburgh, and $600 per year in New York. Milwaukee classifies TV teachers with Master's degrees as Supervising Teachers on its salary schedule. Philadelphia pays $400 above salary to temporary TV teachers, and has a schedule for permanent TV teachers from $11,000 to $17,000. Buffalo schools pay standard salaries, to which the community station WNED-TV (operated by the Western N. Y. ETV Association) adds $50 per produced lesson.

We were unable to ascertain whether cities paying increments get more, or better, work. Some School TV Directors in cities which do not sweeten pay checks say that recruitment of candidates for TV teaching jobs is something of a problem.

Residual rights are a persistent question. Boston's **21-Inch Classroom** pays teachers royalties from syndicated series. Standards for the compensation of **school television** talent, based on responsibilities and experience, appear desirable.

Some ETV stations go **outside school teaching staffs** for their instructor-performers. Three pre-school series which have received strong acceptance (Buffalo's MR. WHATNOT, Memphis' ALL ABOARD WITH MR. B., and WETA-Washington, D.C.'s ROUNDABOUT) chose "warm, male human beings" as interlocutors. KQED, San Francisco, retained Dr. William Martin of Holt, Rinehart & Winston, Inc. in New York as "the best person in the whole country" for a Literature program.

Relationships between TV teachers and their colleagues can, but need not, be tenuous or difficult. In interviews, several school staff people spoke sardonically of "Master Teachers," or voiced disapproval of a "star system." As many as two-thirds of current TV teachers periodically visit classrooms to assess reactions and correspond with classroom teachers. In addition to planning committee sessions, Detroit organizes large meetings with as many as 100 or more teachers for whom a series is being designed; they work out specific problems before a lesson plan is final.

Many classroom teachers said they need to receive their lesson guides months earlier than they now get them. They want to preview programs before they are telecast to their classes. Two Great Cities in 1966-67 regularly scheduled advance telecasts for teachers.

Producers, artists & technicians. Most school systems or ETV stations in the Great Cities have from one to six Producer-Directors, two artists, and photographic assistance. Technical staff tends increasingly to consist of union crews supported by student assistants. There is national need for trained production personnel

TABLE E

ORIGINAL BROADCAST PROGRAMMING
COMPARATIVE OUTPUT BY CITIES — 1966-67*

City	%
Detroit	23.6%
Philadelphia	9.7
Memphis	7.1
Chicago	6.7
St. Louis	6.5
Pittsburgh	6.1
Los Angeles	6.0
San Francisco	5.9
New York	5.7
Cleveland	5.2
Buffalo	4.3
Milwaukee	4.2
Baltimore	3.2
San Diego**	2.9
Boston	2.9
Washington, D. C.	---
	100%***

*Excluding repeats.
**Broadcasting began in February, 1967.
***100% equals 5311 hours.

Sources: The Individual City Public School Systems and EVT Stations

and technicians. This is now met locally by the Milwaukee Technical and Vocational Schools, the John A. O'Connell Vocational High & Technical Institute in San Francisco, the Ampex Institute in Chicago, the George Westinghouse Vocational High School and the commercial RCA Institute in New York. The broadcasting department of the City College of San Francisco has courses in production methods, with use of three CCTV systems serving about half of 9,000 students.

Production and Transmission Facilities

For our purpose here, broadcasting means open circuit transmission that most consumer television sets receive. "Narrowcasting" covers those closed television systems whose signals require special receivers (2,500-megacycles) or connecting cables (CCTV).

Broadcasting (VHF and UHF). Physical plants divide into four rough groupings: (I) the super-duper situations enjoyed by three ETV stations: Boston's WGBH, Chicago's WTTW, and Cleveland's WVIZ, and two school stations, Milwaukee's WMVS and the new New York Board of Education station WNYE; (II) the middle-class conditions which Memphis' WKNO, Philadelphia's WHYY, St. Louis' KETC, San Diego's KEBS, San Francisco's KQED, and Washington's WETA have; (III) the crowded and cramped quarters from which Buffalo's WNED, Detroit's WTVS, and Pittsburgh's WQED manage to function; and (IV) Baltimore, which has no facilities, dependent upon charity. The new State-owned network comes into being in a year or two, and Baltimore school administrators hope they will benefit from the State production center there.

These classifications were accurate in the summer of 1967. But change is the one certain constant in **School Television.** When Boston's WGBH had rented quarters above a bowling alley, it was a threadbare vagrant. After a fire destroyed its few belongings, a successful fund drive made its new building and entirely new equipment possible. Dr. Ohrenberger said this was "falling into a sewer and coming up wearing a top hat." Pittsburgh and San Francisco plan to construct new operating complexes. Washington has just expanded its building. St. Louis has been given equipment by CBS. Buffalo, New York, and San Francisco have first-rate studio equipment but paltry space where their producers, directors and TV teachers work.

Trends are toward use of UHF, more powerful signals, and color. Boston plans to shift all **school television** from VHF Channel 2 to UHF Channel 44. Pittsburgh's ETV station has both VHF and UHF channels which extend the amount of school programming it can offer. UHF requires more power. St. Louis expects soon to have nearly trebled power. Cleveland's new transmitting tower, double the height of the present one, is to be in service by 1968, and transmitting power will increase from 350 to 700 kw.

Eight Great Cities—Baltimore, Boston, Memphis, Milwaukee, Philadelphia, Pittsburgh, San Francisco, and Washington—had varying degrees of color capability, color capable studio and/or transmission equipment. National Educational Television (NET) and the National Center for School and College Television series are now being produced in color.

There are no—repeat, no—correlations established between quality of work, extent of use, and learning results on one hand, and the cities' technical facilities. We could support Parkinson's last Law—that an institution starts its descent as soon as its people become comfortable—by selecting examples of creative imagination from Groups III and IV, or unfairly fixing upon indifferent results where telecasters have the best of circumstances and tools. Or vice versa. **School Television** does not work either way, yet. We saw enough of triumph and fiasco in all four categories. At this stage, **what is done about curriculum, programs, and receivers matters more than the comparatively fine, average or poor space, hardware and power output.**

Of more value to U.S. urban schooling is knowledge of their shared strengths and flaws. Dismal as the extent and sensitivity of their receiving systems may be, all Great Cities have means for transmission that send forth signals up to rigorous FCC standards. There are educators, producers, directors, and engineers who put out acceptable material once they obtain clear specifications on what is required. Many tapes they make are, however, incompatible. Neither Cleveland nor San Diego can directly use what teachers at the Byrd School in Chicago do.

You can see St. Louis' superb HARD TIMES AND GREAT EXPECTATIONS telecast in Washington or Chicago, but not through the facilities of WNYE in New York.

Technical and logistical factors are soluble. These should never impede what schoolmen must do. Still, technological standards for **compatible equipment** are badly needed rules-of-the-road, if equipment manufacturers are to help—rather than hinder—the cities' schools from drawing upon each others' best skills. And more secure experience with all the new media is necessary if schools are not going to waste their scarce money, or others' funds, on equipment which cannot perform as represented, or is not capable of use and punishment in classrooms and broadcast stations without breakdown or excessive maintenance.

"Narrowcasting" (ITFS & CCTV). The most frequently mentioned deterrents to the use of **School Television** were (a) the insufficiency of programs to meet diverse needs, and (b) scheduling. Neither of these constraints can be met without more channels: principally through Instructional Television Fixed Service (ITFS), 2,500-megacycle bands and/or Closed Circuit (CCTV) coupled with videotape recorders to receive and replay telecast programs in each building at will.

ITFS. Detroit is the only Great City system with 2,500-megacycle channels in use. The Cleveland Board of Education filed application for four channels in April, 1967. While Pittsburgh and Philadelphia have had engineering studies made, by August, 1967 no other Great City Public School System had made formal application to the Federal Communications Commission to reserve channels for possible future use. San Francisco has contracted for an ITFS feasibility study.

In four Great Cities' areas there are now from two to 24 2,500-megacycle operations on the air, according to the FCC. In five more Great City areas the FCC has received applications requesting three to 34 channels for their zones. (See Appendix E).

Competition for 2,500-megacycle licenses is growing faster than several Great City school systems appreciate. Why? In several cities, key administrators had never heard of ITFS, or had so little information that what they knew was of scant value. Some welcomed the news of its existence. The FCC and its regional ITFS committees are prepared to consider revising allocations in areas where all 31 channels have been assigned. Normally, any bona fide educational organization may request four. Philadelphia has an extensive plan, anticipating the use of eight channels.

In October, 1967, the Archdiocese of Milwaukee was starting construction of a 4-channel system to embrace 250 schools over a 4,000 square mile area, with installation costs anticipated at $1.5 million.

The Advisory Committee on ETV of the Higher Education Coordinating Council of Metropolitan St. Louis seeks maximum ITFS use. It begins work with a North Circle plan prepared for a group of suburban county school systems. Tentative assignment would be 20 channels to 96 district school systems, four to Catholic schools, one to the Lutheran Synod, four to 31 colleges and universities, and one to miscellaneous agencies with eligible training programs.

Cleveland's educational television station, WVIZ-TV, is to administer operation of the several 2,500-megacycle channels of the Public Schools, the Archdiocese, suburban Palma, and the station's four ITFS bands.

CCTV. Our limited time permitted inquiry into examples of closed circuit arrangements involving only 89 schools in eight Great Cities.

In fall, 1967, Chicago expanded its cluster system begun at Richard E. Byrd Elementary School in 1962 to five clusters, which total 26 public and 16 non-public schools under an ESEA Title I grant. Each cluster now has a studio school, three full-time TV teachers in Science and other "specialty" areas. Regular teachers do much of the on-camera teaching, returning to their home classrooms after televising certain lessons. Since many pupils' families move from one address to another within the same neighborhood cluster, this system helps mitigate some disadvantages of high pupil mobility.

We heard one story told about different children in three cities: each was about a child who was found unreachable, until he or she recognized a teacher on television. In one case the pupil rushed up and kissed the screen. In another, the first words the child said in class were, "My teacher moved with me."

Cleveland has CCTV systems in three buildings: Collinwood and Glenville Sr. and Mooney Jr. High Schools. Also the Supplementary Educational Center.

Detroit has ten schools with operable CCTV. Its Osborn High School was planned to be the nucleus of a cluster joined to feeder schools, but shortage of funds forbade cable connections. Osborn, and Spain

Junior High School have vigorous faculty and student participation, using CCTV to orient all students at the start of each school year, especially for recruiting newcomers for extra-curricular clubs and teams.

All Detroit's new secondary schools constructed in recent years provide for CCTV outlets in every classroom. The newest—Kettering and Manning Wright—have multi-media rooms with provision for computer-assisted instruction, TV, overhead, rear-vision, and conventional projectors. Denby, an older high school, is the only one with its own videotape recorder; purchase of its CCTV was initiated by the faculty, Student Council, and Mothers Club fund-raising activity, aided by the Board of Education.

Not all the Detroit CCTV systems approach full use. The new teacher contract limits work to five classes and one duty unless there is added compensation. Added pay is unlikely. At this writing in late October, Detroit still does not have a firm 1967-68 school budget. TV teacher is considered a separate duty. It may be possible to arrange for a TV coordinator to take certain teachers' classes while they prepare and present lessons over TV.

For the past year Philadelphia has had 34 CCTV units in operation. Its old Conwell School is one of eight "magnet" schools which serves its neighborhood as well as students bussed from other districts. It has a lowered (26/1) pupil-teacher ratio, team teaching, specialized personnel, copious new materials, and innovative ideas. Renovated large rooms have 125 pupils, five teachers, and four to five TV sets. The CCTV system uses a camera and video tape recorder which teachers and pupils use for making tapes and for retrieval and playback of city-wide telecast series. The coordinator is technically a non-professional person, a competent housewife. Teachers told us they regularly use the equipment to develop lessons with the help of outside consultants, and to present them.

Pittsburgh's $120 million plan for five Great High Schools visualizes communications centers with computers, CCTV production facilities and distribution systems, and multi-media centers combining libraries with audio-visual materials and equipment.

Cleveland's Glenville High School, San Diego's Morse High School, the O'Connell Vocational High School and City College in San Francisco all stress training for work in electronic equipment and communications jobs. They also use their CCTV systems as conduits for other teaching, for in-service teacher education, and for supplementary enrichment of curricula.

All new New York schools being built have provision for CCTV distribution ducts and conduits. The city now has eight CCTV systems: In Public School 33 in Manhattan, which until 1961 was linked to four 11- to 22-storey low-rent John Lovejoy Elliott public housing units, the Lower West Side Health Center and the originating Hudson Neighborhood Guild, a settlement house; P.S. 81 and P.S. 86, Bronx; George Westinghouse Vocational & Technical High School, Samuel J. Tilden High School, and P.S. 289 in Brooklyn; P.S. 31 in Bayside, and Junior High School 218 in Flushing. We were disappointed to learn that most of these CCTV systems are lingering remnants of the P.S. 33 Project, using minimum rigs bought for its work. The last two schools listed have some vitality, serving as campus schools for Queens College teacher training.

In the summer of 1967 San Diego had CCTV outlets installed in two of its high schools, and has budgeted $20,000 for lease of videotape recorders for use in secondary schools. Initial purpose is to record and play back telecast series at times of the schools' choosing, thereby helping to overcome scheduling problems.

One city's experience with a junior high school is a regrettable case history. It has a CCTV system which never had a chance to function properly, "designed" by architects who relied on a supplier. They provided two large industrial cameras without a switcher, five wireless microphones only three of which could be used at any one time because of frequency interferences, a videotape recorder incapable of feeding a steady picture to three large screen projectors, and no centralized control facilities. The school system has since rejected proposed additional CCTV installations, on the ground that they should not be approved until the TV system proves its value. This is an actuarially improbable expectation. We were astonished to find that, even with such a grab-bag of components, home-made adaptations permitted the school's people to invent uses for instruction, particularly for in-service training. This, and other experiences like it, point to the need for professional standards and a checklist for CCTV specifications.

TELEVISION RECEIVERS PER 500 ELEMENTARY PUPILS

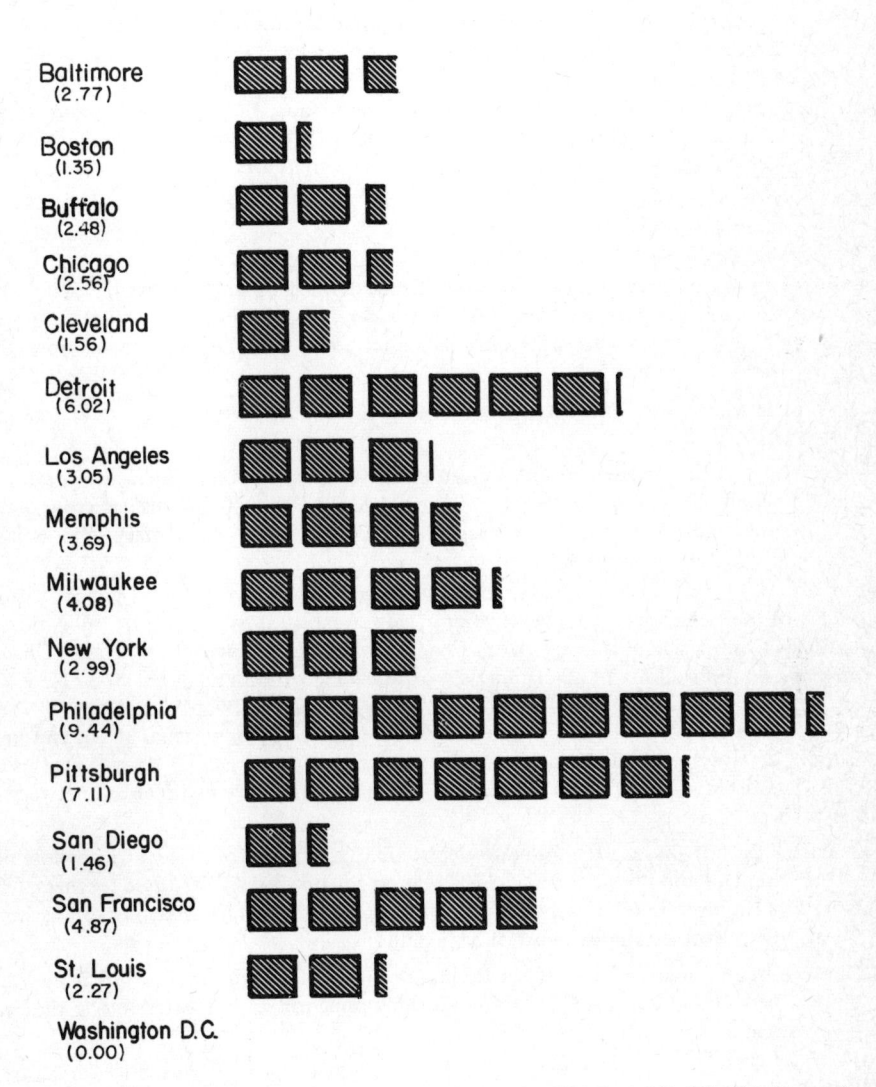

Baltimore (2.77)
Boston (1.35)
Buffalo (2.48)
Chicago (2.56)
Cleveland (1.56)
Detroit (6.02)
Los Angeles (3.05)
Memphis (3.69)
Milwaukee (4.08)
New York (2.99)
Philadelphia (9.44)
Pittsburgh (7.11)
San Diego (1.46)
San Francisco (4.87)
St. Louis (2.27)
Washington D.C. (0.00)

SOURCES: The Individual City Public School Systems

Figure 10

Perishable opportunities. One new resource which suburban and rural towns are exploiting is the offering being made by private CATV (Community Antennas connected to residences and places of business by cable) companies to provide coaxial cable connections to schools without charge. Detroit and St. Louis ETV stations hope to sell school and public television programs to these firms. CATV corporations are now seeking franchises in dense metropolitan areas. Great City school systems can benefit if their city governments grant franchises conditional upon cable connections and reserved channels (which number from 6 to 24, depending on system design) for every public school building in the affected neighborhoods.

Chicago is contemplating extending the Byrd School Cluster's transmission by cable to high-rise apartment buildings. It should seize advantage of hard-won experience with difficulties encountered in New York's P.S. 33 pilot project programming to the high-rise Elliott housing units. While the latter program has not continued according to its original plan, it gained information of practical value.

The Model Cities' program envisions large-scale construction of multiple dwellings. The Great Cities' school systems should explore possibilities for the low-cost apartments to have ducts and conduits for CCTV tied in with school buildings. After mortar is set, CCTV arrangements would be far more costly. The prospects for mutual education between school and community through CCTV can be enormous, if foresight is exercised.

Receiving Equipment and Its Condition

No Great City meets the two alternative desiderata defined by educational telecasters: either one TV set for every 15 students, or no more than one viewer per inch of TV tube size, i.e., 19 pupils for one set with a 19 inch screen, 21 pupils for a 21 inch screen, etc. For most city classrooms now, these standards would require two or three TV sets.

Except for anomalous experimental situations, no principal or teacher we interviewed said there were nearly enough sets.

Distribution of sets is extremely unbalanced in most cities. In June, 1967 New York counted 3,574 sets in 500 of its 634 elementary schools. One school had 40 sets. 270 schools had from one to three sets. 23 schools had none. Boston Public Schools report 150 TV sets in 148 elementary schools and "about 50" in its 36 junior and senior high schools.

A raw census of sets ignores whether they are capable of receiving school telecasts. Boston teachers say that many of their receivers are inoperative or of poor quality. Boston's WGBH Educational Foundation plans eventually to shift school telecasts from Channel 2 (VHF, received by all sets) to Channel 44 (UHF) which can only be received by an all-channel set or older set with an adapter. When New York Board of Education telecasts moved from WNDT's Channel 13 (VHF) to the Board's own new WNYE Channel 25 (UHF), at least 338 school sets were found unable to receive the new signal at all, and in 21 out of 30 school districts the average rated reception was between 1 (not usable) and 2 (fair). New sets obtained with ESEA funds ranged between 3.0 (good) up to 3.2 (4 is excellent) in five districts and between 2.0 (fair) and 2.8 in nine districts.

New York does not present the ultimate electronic vacuum. It is one Great City whose personnel have calibrated the extent of the problem and found, that to get one TV set for three teachers, its schools need 10,576 more sets to cover 35,621 classrooms. To provide master antenna systems in 350 schools—one-third of its buildings—New York estimates a cost of $1.5 million.

Because of great scarcity of TV sets in the junior and senior high schools, much transmission to secondary schools may, for practical use, be considered tooling-up activity prior to the time when the programs can be seen and heard.

Maintenance is an inescapable factor. The best reports on prompt correction of faulty sets were in Memphis—which sends a repair man who usually fixes a troubling or defunct receiver on the spot, and always provides a set in good working order the same day notification is received. Los Angeles, which has a large repair facility, renders completed service within 24 hours. New York authorizes principals to get service from local repair shops. Most vocational high schools provide courses in TV repair. We found only Los Angeles which tied vocational instruction specifically and successfully to the need for fixing school TV sets.

TELEVISION RECEIVERS PER 500 SECONDARY PUPILS

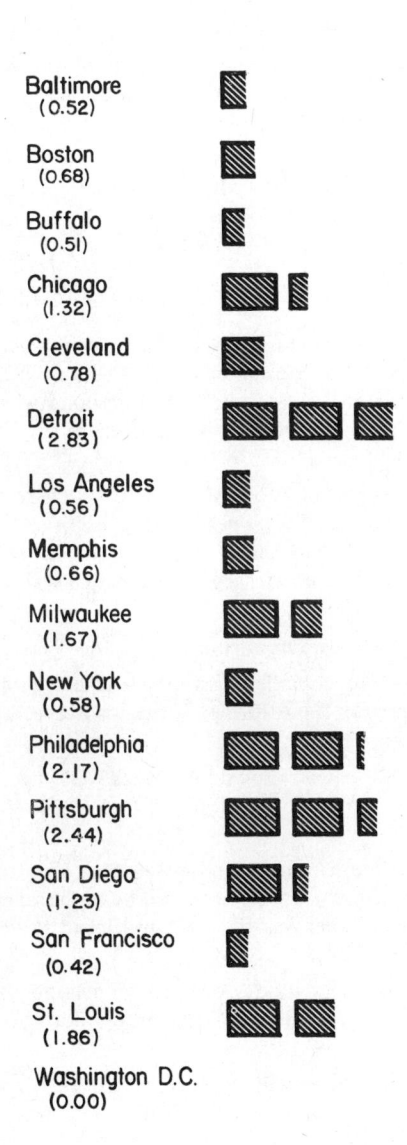

Baltimore (0.52)
Boston (0.68)
Buffalo (0.51)
Chicago (1.32)
Cleveland (0.78)
Detroit (2.83)
Los Angeles (0.56)
Memphis (0.66)
Milwaukee (1.67)
New York (0.58)
Philadelphia (2.17)
Pittsburgh (2.44)
San Diego (1.23)
San Francisco (0.42)
St. Louis (1.86)
Washington D.C. (0.00)

SOURCES: The Individual City Public School Systems

Figure II

Thefts cause grievous losses of sets. Philadelphia inhibits stealing. It buys receivers which have no off-the-air reception capability and can get signals only from outlets connected to the schools' master antennas. Bulk purchasing there, incidentally, is at $99 per set.

Color is a persistent question. Numerous administrators and principals told us that with the increase of color TV sets in homes, including those of the poor, classrooms should have sets as good as their pupils watch at home. The firm trend in purchase of home receivers is toward color. Even though instructional films offered in black-and-white cost half as much, their color prints outsell them. Should school systems undertaking large-scale long-range programs of receiver purchases put substantial sums into black-and-white equipment which may have to be replaced?

Baltimore and Philadelphia are among the cities which have acquired limited numbers of color TV sets.

Learning advantages of color transmission for Art and Science demonstrations seem obvious, even though research designed to find out if color improves learning has yielded contradictory findings. Schools with active parent and neighborhood associations may be the first to replace their black-and-white sets.

Whether in color or black-and-white, planners of instructional materials expenditures are still a long way from providing each classroom with a TV set, every building with a master antenna, and enough spare receivers to assure clear and virtually uninterrupted reception of televised lessons.

Information on Use

What the cities know about their **use of School Television** is meager. When Murphy and Gross wrote, in **Learning by Television**, that "The size and composition of ITV's audience are at best an informed estimate," they were being kind. This Study found that use data in 1966-67 did not correspond with what the Great Cities must have if they are to know how or whether **school television** will meet the acute needs their people identified.

First is whether they relate the question, **Who is viewing?** to obvious factors such as the availability of sets. The scant number of Boston viewers results from one TV set per building (with direct current requiring A.C. converters), and its sets often being so old they cannot tune to the relevant instructional programs on the parochial schools' UHF channel (being shifted to 2,500-megacycles). **School TV** thus could not offer Boston city pupils much.

Next is that **"utilization"** surveys are largely quantitative head-counts.

The nearly universal practice in Great Cities is to compile classroom teachers' replies to questionnaires. Most teachers we interviewed have little use for these forms. Those who take the questionnaires seriously tend to express unrepresentative praise or gripes.

Some of the questionnaires appear to ask good questions. They do not work well in getting particularly useful answers. The two best procedures we saw were applied by Boston's **21 Inch Classroom** and Memphis' WKNO.

Boston's **21 Inch Classroom** tabulates answers from returned questionnaires on punch cards. Rudimentary programming permits print-outs by city and town, by schools, and by series, on regular and occasional use, reactions, and numbers of viewing classes. This was the most proficient use of what is still a blunt instrument—the printed questionnaire.

Another method is to count the number of teachers' guides ordered by school systems. This is a coarse measuring stick. Quite a few teachers told us they used the guides, but did not tune to the televised fare.

The Memphis Junior League conducts depth interviews with teachers. These gather potentially valuable reactions and suggestions which, if implemented by the administrators, could surely contribute to learning results.

No method we found in current use comes to grips with the major question, whether the students are finding the televised lessons useful for their learning. Better information should come from the teachers, pupils, and subject area supervisors working closely with coordinators in each school building.

DETERRENTS TO MORE EFFECTIVE USE OF BROADCAST TELEVISION BY CITY

	PROGRAM CONTENT	RECEPTION	SCHEDULING	TEACHER USE	TIME, STAFF, MONEY	POLICY	
Baltimore	6	11	7	3	1	2	30
Boston	9	5	1	4	1	2	22
Buffalo	9	5	3	5	1	—	23
Chicago	2	—	3	1	1	—	7
Cleveland	11	14	6	2	1	—	34
Detroit	3	5	7	7	—	2	24
Los Angeles	11	11	10	13	2	—	47
Memphis	4	3	4	2	—	—	13
Milwaukee	11	1	4	6	2	—	24
New York	2	5	8	4	5	—	24
Philadelphia	2	—	1	9	4	1	17
Pittsburgh	7	11	10	4	2	3	37
San Diego	2	9	6	8	2	—	27
San Francisco	12	10	8	1	3	—	34
St. Louis	14	18	7	5	—	4	48
Wash. D.C.	—	—	—	—	—	—	—
No. of Responses out of 218 Interviews	105	98	85	74	25	14	401

- Most frequently mentioned deterrent
- 2nd most frequently mentioned deterrent
- 3rd " " " " " " "

Figure 12

Research. Time and again we found highly qualified departments of research in the Great Cities, whose experience and skills were not being applied to curricular research on the use of **School Television**, or the learning results from multi-media approaches. This is all wrong. There is not nearly enough pertinent, useful research being done.

Use of non-instructional TV. Administrative TV programs also get simplistic estimates of audience size. Opinion research, determining what municipal, State, and other decision-makers know about school conditions, problems, and needs, could aid in telling what areas of ignorance and understanding require most effort. For two-way communication, such polls can help key officials know more about what parents and voters think, feel, and want. Internal uses of **school TV** might benefit from more knowledge of classroom teachers' thinking for Superintendents' guidance. Adult education, we were told frequently, must learn more about its markets if it is going to reach them effectively.

4. **Constraints**

What factors deter **School Television** from making a larger contribution to instruction in the Great Cities?

Responses to this query correspond to most of the factors listed earlier as the most acute instructional problems, although with different weighting:

(a) With varied phasing 105 reactions were that **program** content is not relevant to urban children or to the school system's curriculum, that programs are not creative enough, or that they are too difficult or too easy for pupils at different ability levels in particular subjects.

School TV personnel cannot assume responsibilities of the Superintendent, Board, and other administrators. It is not up to telecasters to reform the curriculum. **School Television**, with other media, can be a catalyzing instrument for transforming content and method when the responsible policy makers and instructional officers decide what content and method shall be.

The widely-iterated assertion that most ITV is mediocre is at once a careless oversimplification, telling more about the critics than their quarry, and a canard.

Curriculum and programs challenging the capacity of today's youngsters are more easily prescribed than delivered. We noted certain new approaches which bear on curricular problems of inner-city youth as well as of the unmotivated fortunate. Detroit's CABBAGES AND KINGS, a junior high school Humanities series, presents the classic riches of Mark Twain and Thoreau along with works of contemporary creators such as Disney, Ellison, and Richard Wright . . . limiting most sequences in any program to the attention span of a rock-and-roll record. San Diego's PROCESS TO PRODUCT (since retitled CROSSROADS, A LESSON IN INQUIRY) presents problems which do not have any one "correct" answer, inviting reasoning based upon observation of phenomena; the student's hypothesis could be as valid as the teacher's, or anyone else's. This series also had research procedures for evaluation of different kinds of learning results an integral part of its conceptual purpose.

From the suggestions and proposals advanced by scores of Great Cities' school people, we are sure that the educational talent to provide increasingly better programs is abundant, if there are the conditions and resources with which to work.

(b) There were 98 complaints about **reception**. Time and again we were told that TV sets were unavailable, or so scarce that getting to use them was too difficult, or antenna sensitivity or signal strength were too poor for viewing.

(c) **Scheduling** was the third most frequently cited barrier. 85 responses said that a teacher cannot tune to what she wants when she wants it.

Even if there were instant assemblage of more broadcast channels, ITFS 2,500-megacycle channels, CCTV clusters, videotape recorders in every building, and several TV sets were in every classroom, these additions would not automatically resolve scheduling differences.

Bell systems vary from school to school. In one city we saw a meticulous chart. It showed, conclusively, that **very** rarely could any telecast program reach a list of schools and have its start and end come

TABLE F

REPORTED BUDGETED EXPENDITURES FOR SCHOOL TELEVISION IN GREAT CITIES, 1966-67*

	Net Local Funds	Federal Grants*	State Aid	Total
Baltimore	$ 150,254	$ 27,452	$	$ 177,706
Boston	42,000			42,000
Buffalo	25,200	100,000	10,800	136,000
Chicago	188,420	395,000		583,420
Cleveland	127,375		32,625	160,000
Detroit	428,600	393,995		822,595
Los Angeles	233,259		152,711	385,970
Memphis	100,000	N.A.		100,000
Milwaukee	123,000	6,900		129,900
New York	688,523	3,840	50,000	742,363
Philadelphia	875,000	600,000		1,475,000
Pittsburgh	117,524	54,950		172,474
St. Louis	100,000			100,000
San Diego	50,000		50,000	100,000
San Francisco	35,505		28,975	64,480
Washington, D. C.				
Totals	$3,284,660	$1,582,137	$325,111	$5,191,908

*These Federal Grants are for special projects in 1966-67 and are not a part of the normal school budget.

Sources: The Individual City Public School Systems.

within class periods at most of the schools. This suggests that, for the success of any new curricular services, the principals' involvement is as necessary as any technology.

(d) 74 responses put the blame for inadequate **use** of programs upon the **teachers**, whose pre-service preparation and in-service education are not up to today's needs, and said there is a virtual absence of communication between classroom and TV teachers.

In cities where we found fewer, or less strenuous, complaints from teachers and principals, there appeared to be more involvement in selecting series from outside resources, or in the planning, production, and introduction of locally originated series.

(e) There were 25 respondents who felt that **money** was insufficient for getting enough good programs and more extensive use. We found only moderate correlation between investment per elementary pupil and reported regular elementary school use.

The things that money can buy: more personnel time for substantially better scripts, for obtaining visual and sound components, for rehearsal, and for editing, are needed in all Great Cities. Qualified staff exists; if it were stretched less thinly over too much to do, quality output should improve. More money and better methods for making sure that the cities get their money's worth are imperative.

(f) 14 replies said their school system's administrative **policies** were indefinite, lukewarm, or did not encourage use of TV on a scale comparable to its potentials. So far as we could tell in the summer of 1967, this was the case in at least 14 Great Cities.

Some 30 other constraints were mentioned more than once. In four cities—Boston, Cleveland, New York, and St. Louis—repair service needs improving. Cleveland, Milwaukee, Pittsburgh, and Los Angeles people want program schedules and teachers' guides sooner in the school year. Memphis and Milwaukee respondents would like less lecturing and more vivid visual material on their TV screens. In Detroit and St. Louis school buildings were said to be architecturally unsuited to television. The balance of interview answers were largely local or personal objections to TV teachers' teaching, classroom teachers' dislike (abruptly so among older secondary instructors) of television altogether, and programs considered too long, too short, dull, or passive.

5. Costs

Reports from the Great Cities school systems show they attributed about $5.2 million to **School Television** expense in 1966-67. Of this, approximately $1.6 million came from federal grants and $325,111 in state aid. The $3.3 million from local funds is less than 0.16% of these cities' total operating school budgets of roughly $3.4 billion.

One of our group familiar with accepted industry cost analysis noted that these figures did not include many actual costs incurred in rendering **School Television** service. Even so, it is highly probably that these services actually cost the cities at least $10 million. Three generalizations are certainties:

(a) In terms of budgetary commitments, the Boards and Superintendents did not depend on **School TV** for significant help in meeting their most acute problems.

(b) Its real costs are not known.

(c) It is unclear what effective results were obtained and at what prices.

Cost data are inconsistent and incomplete. Few ETV Managers keep track of past grants for capital equipment. We obtained better information from federal agencies and the Ford Foundation than from these sources. Few ETV stations or **School TV** units know how much their individual series and programs cost. Not many of their administrators have anything to do directly with procurement and maintenance of equipment, or CCTV operations. Some cities put certain equipment in operating budgets. Others do not. None amortizes large capital acquisitions which inevitably require replacement. Overhead is ignored.

There are good local reasons why nearly every Great City has its own system for counting costs. However, on **School Television** there are numerous reasons for translating them into a standard accounting practice. Aside from possible future large-scale federal support of non-profit TV, such "equilibrated" cost data would be useful: for avoiding unwitting subsidy when applying for federal and other grants, negotiating

TABLE G

EXPENDITURES FOR SCHOOL TELEVISION*
1966-67

CITY	PER ENROLLED PUPIL Elementary	Secondary	BUDGETED EXPENDITURES
Baltimore	$ .93	$ .62	$ 150,254
Boston	.65	.25	42,000
Buffalo	.61	.27	36,000
Chicago	.38	.18	188,420
Cleveland	.93	1.40	160,000
Detroit	1.81	.94	428,600
Los Angeles	.88	.80	385,970
Memphis	1.41	.09	100,000
Milwaukee	1.27	.29	123,000
New York	.71	.66	738,523
Philadelphia	3.78	2.39	875,000
Pittsburgh	1.63	1.13	117,524
St. Louis	.56	1.98	100,000
San Diego	.79	.86	100,000
San Francisco	.96	.36	64,480
Washington, D. C.	—	—	0
AVERAGE (15 cities)	$1.15	$ .82	$3,609,771

*Does not include federal grants.

Sources: The Individual City Public School Systems.

cooperative arrangements through ETV associations also serving other systems, setting rates for rental of series the cities produce, and fair division of responsibility in cooperative undertakings by two or more school systems.

The most important reason is to get a clear base for making choices among various instructional media for particular tasks: comparison of true costs with results sought (and, when ascertainable, the learning results obtained) with the money. To presume that precise cost-effectiveness procedures are attainable for use of multi-media, or of any individual medium, in any Great City in 1967 would be ingenuous. A clearer view, to guide planning and decisions, than now exists is both possible and necessary.

How much difference would more money mean toward overcoming major constraints? Enough TV sets and better antennas would improve poor reception. More channels, CCTV systems, and videotape recorders would obviate some, but not all scheduling difficulties. Money alone would **not**, necessarily, ensure improved program relevance, teachers' use of series, or administrative attitudes. But these deterrents should be diluted if there were more substantial commitment to television as part of more relevant curriculum, while using constellations of many new and "old" media.

Counsels of perfection could be idle. Large sums are being spent, however, in what is necessarily an evolution toward competence for meeting individual student needs on a massive scale. As a way of thinking, so that today's decisions can lead toward a markedly better use of resources, time and talent, we asked authoritative sources **what order of funding for school television would be needed to buy basic physical facilities in the Great Cities?** By basic, we mean those essentials that could enable their school systems to take advantage of the inherent flexibility of the television medium: including programs from and uses of commercial, educational, and instructional television as well as closed transmission systems. We obtained prices for equipment now on the market, for installations that could be begun tomorrow morning.

In 1966-67 we had seen **School Television** used as though the Great Cities had allotted one textbook for each dozen students and one manual for every five teachers. Without dreaming of an optimum situation, we priced what should provide a threshold. The quest was for that critical mass that could change old habits and permit large city school systems more nearly to apply their best present strengths. Even the best informed authorities warned that the following figures are rough, rule of thumb estimates:

1) Supplying every classroom teacher with a black-and-white TV set and stand would be **$150 each**.
2) Putting a coaxial distribution system in every building would be **$80 per classroom**.
3) Supplying every school with two black-and-white videotape recorders with playback would be **$4,000**.
4) Two videcon cameras, a simple switcher, and two microphones with audio switcher would be **$1,600**.
5) Each building's receiving antenna and down converter means **$1,500**.
6) For every Great City to have a four-channel ITFS transmitter would be **$51,000**.
7) For every Great City to have an equipped studio would be **$60,000**.

These would mean access to all broadcast local and syndicated school, educational, and commercial television over VHF, UHF, and the 2,500-megacycle channels as well as CCTV. **The bill** for such physical facilities in every classroom, school, and system in the Great Cities **would be approximately $65 million**. To make system-wide transmission and classroom reception **color capable** would total nearer **$150 million**.

Such expenditures—although only $15 and $35 per pupil—would now be premature. Hardware without substantially more relevant programming (which would cost additionally, in the short run far less, but in the long run more than equipment) would be to multiply more of the same. Either course—in black-and-white or color—would place unearned confidence in any single instructional medium. The expense for saturation uses of available films, filmstrips, transparencies, motion and still picture projectors, and audio equipment at standards comparable to the most successful demonstration programs, for every classroom and school, would be about equal to this threshold use of **School Television** in color. Perhaps Great Cities planners should dare to consider using both options. And all practical alternatives require scrutiny.

6. Summary of Findings

(a) Programs & Uses

Functions
: **School television** in the Great Cities had four major uses: instruction (90.16%); teacher education (5.63%); community information (2.93%); and administrative (1.26%).

Amount of Programming
: Hours of unrepeated telecasting vary from 150 to more than 1,200 per year. The city with the most programming had over double that of the second ranking city, and 8 times as much as the one with the least. In the Great Cities, television programming represented less than 3% of total possible instructional hours.

Use
: Reported regular users ranged from 22% to 94% of elementary, and from less than 1% to 68% of secondary enrollments.

Grade Levels
: Majority of programs were for elementary pupils, with peak at grade 6. Great Cities' programming was about the same as national norm in share of hours for upper elementary and junior high students. The cities allotted more than half again as much for primary grades, and only half that for all U.S. high schools. Elementary programming (K-6) was over twice that of secondary.

Subjects
: Almost two-thirds of the programs fell into four subject areas: Science (19%); Foreign Languages (15%); Social Studies (14%); and English and Language Arts (14%). The subject emphasis resembled national norm with two significant exceptions: Teacher Education (with 4 times as much in the Great Cities) and English and Language Arts (with better than twice as much). Subjects emphasized were those where teachers were said to feel least secure, or where outside resources were of most value.

Pre-school
: There is disagreement on value of TV for pre-K child, but strong consensus on its value for staff development and parent education.

Vocational
: Little use was being made of TV for vocational students, but there is evidence this could be valuable.

Program Sources
: School-produced programs occupied 36% of telecasts. Other local agencies furnished 25%, outside sources about 39%. There is considerable duplication and no significant pattern among the cities on their program sources.

(b) Promising Practices

Local involvement occurs most often in CCTV situations. Collaborative process appears more important than production polish for gaining teacher acceptance. Televised introduction of new curricula to teachers as well as students. Teacher education, with Micro-teaching a basic advance. Administrative, community and adult uses of television are encouraging.

(c) Facilities and Operations

Ownership
: Two cities' schools control channels; 13 contract with ETV, university or commercial stations for school services. ETV stations tend to serve suburbs. Detroit was the only Great City now using 2,500 Mc. channels. Trend is toward "narrowcasting," especially with closed circuit systems run by the Great Cities themselves. In 1966-67 the facilities for **school television** broadcasting were almost entirely outside the control of the Great City School Systems.

Personnel
: Trend is toward integrating supervisory responsibilities for all media. School TV Director usually reports to Instructional Administrator and has but fleeting contact with Superintendent. TV teachers usually have no special professional training as such or recognition; six cities pay them increments. Training of technical personnel a growing need.

Production & Transmission	Trends are toward UHF and closed transmission systems, more power, and color capability. No real correlations between technical adequacy of facilities, program use, or learning results. Few Great Cities are applying for 2,500 Mc. channels. Some provide for CCTV ducts and cables in new buildings.
Receiving Equipment	Supply of TV sets ranges from 1.35 to 9.44 per 500 elementary pupils, and from 0.42 to 2.83 per 500 secondary students. Many sets are old and cannot receive UHF signals. Color is just beginning.
Information on Use	All data attest that there are many school viewers. Within each system there were widely disparate opinions on the amount of use.

(d) **Constraints**

In order of importance, according to number of responses in interviews: relevance of programming (105); reception (98); scheduling (85); poor use (74); inadequate budgets (25); and insufficient administrative support (14).

What is done about curriculum, programs, and receivers matters more than the comparatively fine, average, or poor space, hardware, and power output.

(e) **Costs**

Great Cities reported $5.2 million annual expenditure on TV (though true costs are at least double that) out of a total operating budget of $3.4 billion. **School Television** costs accounted for less than .16% or roughly 1/650 of the total budget. Average costs per pupil in 1966-67: elementary, $1.15; secondary, $.82. The highest combined per-pupil budget (excluding federal grants) was about 10 times the lowest. There is only moderate correlation between investment per pupil, the number of broadcast hours, and reported regular users.

III. SUMMARY & CONCLUSION

1. **Purpose**

The Research Council's Educational Communications Project is a status study of the current use of computers, television, and various instructional materials being used by schools of the Great Cities. The Council's Instructionals Materials Committee approved a position paper of its sub-committee on television, stating that "legislation precipitated by the Carnegie Commission report may result in considerable money for Public Television, but very little for Instructional Television" and that "There is an urgent need for television to be used to upgrade instruction in such areas as:

"The equalization of educational opportunity, especially in large school systems faced with this problem and serving extremely large numbers of pupils.

"The orientation and in-service training of the professional and non-professional staffs of school systems. This is particularly true of large city schools having massive needs for trained personnel.

"The introduction of new teaching methods and techniques which affects the metropolitan schools severely because of the great heterogeneous needs in their large school population."

Among the consultant resources retained by Council Task Forces to conduct the broad status study, the Fund for Media Research undertook to ascertain the status and needs of the schools, as served by television, in the 16 Great City public school systems.

2. **Problem**

An underlying question the Instructional Materials Committee and the Fund for Media Research shared was **Why School Television?** Its corollaries helped unify all other study tasks:

(a) In 1966-67, was television serving the acute instructional needs of Great City public schools? How did the school people define these needs? In what ways did their use of television help meet the priorities as they saw them?

(b) To what extent were these school systems taking advantage of the sharply different **modes** of transmission: channels beamed to all or any grouping of schools, within the confines of one or a few buildings, or to sub-groups within a particular grade level?

(c) How did the school systems employ television in conjunction with their other instructional media?

3. **Procedures**

The Council obtained a planning grant from the U.S. Office of Education for this and other preliminary studies. It held a meeting in St. Louis attended by **School Television** people from Great Cities, who reviewed the Fund's outline plan. The Fund surveyed reports of others' pertinent findings on urban school problems and developments in **School Television**, and sought the guidance of numerous persons of nationally recognized experience with urban schools and/or instructional media. (See Appendix G)

It used three questionnaire instruments: the first gained an array of objective data through mail response; the second two provided structure for 291 interviews with 466 persons at varied levels of responsibility in the 16 Great City schools: Superintendents, administrators, supervisors, principals, teachers, and instructional media people. Three field interviewers and a researcher then sifted, checked, and correlated the factual data with interview responses prior to the drafting of this report.

4. **Conclusion**

Any overview of **School Television** in 1967 should have bifocal lenses: fixing first on what it did, and then on what it did not do. Its work served many valuable purposes. At best, there were new paths blazed in the highest tradition. Its negligence mirrors the larger frustration of city school systems' difficulties in coming to grips with what school people stated were their most acute problems.

These problems as stated in 291 interviews with 466 people are, in ranked order of priority: Curriculum relevance and diversity; Teacher quality and quantity; Interfering environmental realities; Staff workload; Communication within and outside the school system; Administrative leadership and practices; Inadequate and uncertain finances; and Obsolete and insufficient facilities. There is lack of agreement within and among the cities and between people with differing professional responsibilities on the definition and priorities of their acute problems.

School Television is not coming to grips with these problems in any of its major aspects:

(1) The amount and kinds of programming are generally not serving the basic needs of the Great Cities' schools.

(2) Facilities and operations are, for the most part, at the periphery of the school system.

(3) Budget levels reflect low priority consideration.

We are forced to conclude, from this evidence in 1966-67, that—despite the almost universally acclaimed potentials of **School Television**—its role in the Great Cities was supplementary, if not on the fringe. Lack of direction and support, by the schools' leadership, appeared in most instances to be the principal cause.

IV. RECOMMENDATIONS

The Fund for Media Research recommends that the Research Council of the Great Cities instruct all appropriate Council working committees to progress from the principle of cooperative study to help in planning action projects for more relevant use of **School Television**, on which:

(a) individual cities undertake projects using television—in conjunction, where feasible, with other instructional media, including radio — designed to answer their most severe unmet needs, with plans for evaluation and communication of results to other school systems, and

(b) two or more cities participate in cooperative projects with similarly shared evaluation and dissemination of ongoing results.

We believe that committee procedures which the Research Council has found successful for initiating and carrying out studies would be meager for obtaining workable cooperation on the projects we consider desirable. Supervision by committees, however well staffed, is unlikely to get either the needed money or the continuity essential for administrative supervision, particularly on projects which may take three, four, or more years to complete.

We therefore recommend that the Research Council create or retain an **operating** agency, with a high level Board of Directors and suitable advisory committees, to carry out the following initial priority tasks related to the Great Cities' school systems' most acute problems:

1. To plan and help put into action, in at least one but preferably more Great Cities, saturation use of **School Television** for perceived major needs, using combinations of open circuit telecasting, Instructional Television Fixed Service on 2,500 Mc. bands, and closed circuit systems in all suitable school buildings and neighborhood clusters.

    San Francisco was the first Great City to express interest, contingent upon adequate financing. Prospect of funding could improve if one or more other cities also took leadership, and were prepared to seek a mix of private and public support.

2. To plan and carry out, in at least one but preferably more cities, a program of maximum relevance for in-service Urban Teacher Education and staff development, using television and other appropriate media to the utmost extent these tools can serve these cities' particular requirements.

    Cleveland was the first to signify its interest, conditional upon obtaining sufficient funding. Other cities' commitment to parallel programs should be canvassed with inventory of the resources they could bring to a jointly conducted revision of their current practices.

3. To develop specifications and standards for equipment, facilities, and operations by working with school systems, engineering personnel, industry, and professional resources.

4. To devise realistic methods of cost accounting which permit the Great Cities to ascertain their true costs of **School Television** services.

5. To improve upon current reporting and evaluation practices, so that each Great City can have more accurate qualitative and quantitative measures of its **School Television** uses.

6. To extend **School Television** through closed circuits and 2,500 Mc. telecasts to families in multiple dwellings, storefronts, community centers, and premises of service organizations. This advance could tie into plans for Model Cities' programs.

    Chicago and New York have evidenced some interest in projects of this character. It would be useful to have additional cities prepared to experiment. One earlier pilot program proved abortive.

7. To explore and extend administrative uses of television to communicate with and inform school staffs and the community. Gaining productive feedback by telephone from teacher groups attending system-wide faculty meetings would exploit the instancy inherent in this medium.

8. To pool resources for cooperatively sponsored production and exchange of television series and programs. Appendix E of the Fund's Study Report lists several suggestions advanced by Great Cities' school people.

    A most acute need is oral language competence. The director of the Instructional Media Committee's Language Arts Project has expressed interest in the potentials of a television series.

To obtain funding and to administer these action projects, we recommend establishment of a **Great Cities School Television Authority**. It should be responsible to its Board (chosen by the Research Council), work directly with school systems taking part in particular projects, cooperate actively with each pertinent committee of the Research Council, and be a service resource to all Great City member school systems.

Some Benefits of a Cooperative Agency

1. Improved ability for Great Cities to articulate their common equipment and operational requirements, exerting their leverage to spur industrial development. A recent U.S. Commissioner of Education told a Research Council session that school systems should prescribe their own specifications for industry to fill.

There is a neglected, reciprocal dimension. Corporations have shown the Fund innovations on their drawing boards which complement needs that teachers and principals described to our interviewers.

2. Making known to such government agencies as the Federal Communications Commission what special needs the Great Cities have — such as their needs, in some instances, for more than four 2,500 Mc. channels — for formulation of national communications policies.
3. Applications for grant support of projects initiated by individual cities should carry greater weight, for funding by government or private sources, if their application to other Great Cities' needs is clear.
4. A research and development resource for individual city's planning can be more reliable than competing salesmen's claims, and can help anticipate imminent technological developments. A retrieval system for identification of existing visual materials, and procedure for getting them for each city's **School Television** uses, could be valuable.
5. Television series and programs produced under cooperative auspices could be distributed nationally, and yield income to the Research Council through the Authority, helping defray some operational costs. Similarly, the Authority could negotiate rentals and licensing of series, programs, and excerpts from member cities' productions.
6. A framework for intercommunication and joint action can reduce wasteful duplication, and foster practices among all Great Cities after one or more have found them effective.

The Fund for Media Research would welcome the opportunity to continue its work with the Council, for helping put these recommendations into action. The Fund suggests that, as immediate next steps, it serve as a Council resource which will work with Superintendents and Member Districts to:

1. Establish model research and development pilot projects for testing new potentials of television in meeting specific needs within the acute problem areas.
2. Establish the basis for a functional agency that would help carry out, at the national and local levels, the tasks approved by member school systems.

APPENDICES

APPENDIX A

PROPOSALS AND SUGGESTIONS

Made by Great Cities School People

1. For sharing information

    a. An informal group has been exchanging Science scripts.

       Detroit, New York, and Cincinnati take part. A formal framework with all interested Great Cities' Science supervisors could be mutually valuable.

    b. Exchange tapes of each city's series, for screening by ITV planning committees.

    c. A workshop for superintendents and key administrators.

    d. Exchange of information between public information officers on activities which capture and sustain interest of the public in school matters.

    e. Share experience on specific equipment performance.

    f. Survey equipment manufacturers for matching new technological developments with special needs of city schools.

    g. Develop a bibliographic retrieval system for better use of all instructional materials.

    h. An organization for exchanging information among TV teachers, engineers, and other operational personnel.

    i. A manual on what is found to work well and badly in transmitting visual information through various styles of lettering, numerals, and other symbols over television.

2. Development and sharing of talent

    a. Creation of Master Teachers in Urban Education, honoring productive service.

    b. A system for referral and transfer of uncommonly effective teachers between Great Cities. When they move, they should not be lost to urban schools.

    c. A jointly developed program for in-service teacher education, geared to particular inner-city requirements.

    d. A cooperative program for training TV teachers.

    e. Ten Great Cities' directors of research have met twice, in Washington. They have submitted a proposal to the Research Council, recommending cooperative projects in instructional television, pre-kindergarten, remedial reading, and other areas. Needed now are structure, money, and a set of priorities within the special projects to begin work.

    f. A system for training and locating technical personnel.

    g. Training institutes for para-professional teacher aides, community liaison coordinators, and Head Start workers.

3. Development and Sharing of Programs

   a. An in-service teacher education series showing master teachers at work in their classrooms.

   b. Teacher education series on developing rapport with individual students; how to handle discipline problems; techniques for class management; grouping procedures promoting involvement; various methods of presenting concepts and information, and handling special problem children.

   c. Having directors of English, Foreign Languages, Health and Physical Education, History and Social Studies, Mathematics, and Science cooperate through planning and execution of in-service teacher education series.

   d. Because "children live for heroes," having Bob Richards, Jesse Owens, Bill Cosby, Stan Musial, foremost physicians and sociologists share presentations on sportsmanship, family living, sex education, narcotics, vandalism, and other "sensitive" topics.

   e. Develop cooperative TV materials on home economics, civil rights, urban culture for parents, and English as a Second Language.

   f. A cooperative series on language arts for the disadvantaged.

   g. Adult evening programs on consumer education; how to organize your household; family living, including sex education, and basic skills.

   h. Shared production on Health Education series involving nutrition; sleep, rest, and exercise; personal grooming and cleanliness; dental health; conservation of vision and hearing; prevention of disease; social and emotional adjustment; family living; the role of sex in life; and safety.

   i. A jointly produced series on developmental reading.

   j. TV programs for parents on How Can Parents Know Their School, Why School Is Important to Your Children, How to Help Your Child Study, and How to Get Your Children Ready for School.

   k. Exchanging taped and kinescoped series to be screened by local subject area planning committees.

APPENDIX B
EXCERPTS FROM INTERVIEWS

I. THE MOST ACUTE INSTRUCTIONAL PROBLEMS

(1) Curriculum not adapted to the diversity of needs presented by today's city children and adults

"Grades certainly are not enough reward for success at school. They must see **goals** more clearly in terms of end product. TV can bring the work-a-day world before them so that they can see what they are working for. What are the possibilities of what they might want to do with themselves? What does a nurse do? A pilot? A welder? Neither the poor nor the middle class knows what work is."

— A School Board Member

"Betty Furness in the kitchen and the green lawns of the suburbs just aren't going to connect. Textbooks and, for that matter, TV have got to show differently colored people in realistic settings — an urban laundromat, a city street, and the rest."

— A School Board Member

"One of our most acute problems is job preparation. We are comfortable with the academic courses compared with the 'job preparation' task. Perhaps all big cities ought to withdraw from accrediting associations, unless these bodies can develop more realistic standards in line with the needs of our student populations. By and large, we are failing to give adequate training to these youngsters for life in our society. Vocational education should be an integral part of the comprehensive high school, rather than isolated from the mainstream of the curriculum. It costs twice as much to train a student vocationally than it does to prepare him for college."

— A Superintendent

"We need a day high school for adults — the 21 or 19 year olds who should not be mixed in with the 14 and 15 year olds. We could accelerate such a program with a separate site, and with the systematic use of television."

— An Associate Superintendent

"Many of our children simply bring their bodies to school. They have no interest in what we try to teach them. They are in-school dropouts."

— A Supervisor

"I don't like the time-credit straight-jacket. How about taking 20 kids and 2 teachers, and letting them go? This magical Carnegie unit means nothing. Why spend 90 hours on Algebra, when some kids can do it in less than half of that? Why keep kids who can read down in the primary Reading classes? Getting the wraps off kids early enough could significantly decrease the numbers who are emotionally disturbed by the time they reach high school. Class sizes should be appropriate to the learning task: some 200 - 1, and others 1 - 1. Right now it takes seven to ten years for a new idea to get into a secondary textbook."

— A Superintendent

"Even the simplest technological aids, like the slide film, are under-used. The army did a good job. The schools have failed here."

— A Deputy Superintendent

"Today's students no longer accept what their teachers or textbooks say. We must learn how to teach current issues that are relevant to current needs. More mature content is needed. Textbooks alone cannot do. The quality of ITV should make them discriminating viewers."

— A Director of Secondary Education

"The children in my sixth grade have little understanding of what the rest of the world is about. One day we talked about going to the moon in a rocket. I asked the class how big the moon is. Some children thought it was as big as the room. Some thought it about as big as a city block. The largest any of them thought was about as big as Milwaukee."

— A Teacher

"We have to learn how to get kids and teachers turned on. The kids need feelings of self-worth and esteem. One essential ingredient is the attitude on the teachers' part that they believe the kids can learn and they can convince the kids they believe this. It's so absurdly simple."

— A Superintendent

"The most acute instructional problem is that the disadvantaged tend to retrogress in learning at about the third or fourth grade, particularly in Reading."

— A Curriculum Specialist & Coordinator

"One of the youngsters' greatest needs is someone who will listen to them and try to understand them."

— A Principal

"We are not making progress in academic achievement as a city, a large city, that we should."

— A Superintendent

"The whole area of adult basic education is at the point where Columbus was in the middle of the ocean. It hasn't even been discovered yet."

— A Director of Extension Education

"We must make room and time for television in schools. We will have to take a new look at our curriculum, and get some of the unessentials out of the traditional curriculum, making room for the new which will replace it."

— A Principal

"Public school systems are still too textbook-oriented, while today's kids are not. Society is moving at tremendous speed; teaching is not."

— A Director of Community Relations

"Teaching kids to read, write and figure — the basic skills — is what we're doing lousiest at."

— A Superintendent

(2) Teacher quality and quantity

"No teacher-training institution is preparing its teachers for the inner city. The professors tiptoe into the inner city, and then scurry back to their ivory tower."

— A Superintendent

"We had many resignations of elementary teachers in the wake of the riots last summer. They just want to get out. Besides, many of the best teachers are being grabbed up by colleges who want first-rate teachers with inner-city teaching experience. Colleges are not training teachers adequately."

— A Superintendent

"Teachers should go off with a policeman on the beat, a visiting nurse, a social worker. They need to see how their kids really live. Middle class teachers aren't exposed to the seamier side of life. We need to take teachers to the kids' environment, to see what life is like when things are tough. They should go to their pupils' churches. There is a spirit there that the teachers never get."

— A School Board Member

"When you bring a new tool into our school, don't assume teachers know anything about it. You will be more successful with in-service training if you start from scratch."

— A Teacher

"Teacher-training institutions are not with it. They are still 25 years behind the times. They should incorporate more educational technology into their pre-service program."

— A Deputy Superintendent

"If we continue to have trouble in getting qualified teachers, we should make more use of technology to spread the talent of our best teachers."

— A Superintendent

"Cut down on the theory. Show us, basically and simply, how you do it. We'll find things to do with it if we know what it is for."

— A Teacher

"I would welcome new teachers to help my older teachers get zipped up. The younger ones have a lot more vitality."

— A Principal

"This year 10 of my 35 teachers are new. Four are Liberal Arts majors. We need a definitive city-wide in-service training program."

— A Principal

"The teachers' institutes are a joke."

— An Assistant Superintendent

"My faculty is old. It has become inbred and got into ruts. One of my biggest problems is protecting the children from the teachers."

— A Principal

"We have to restructure the use of teachers. Possibly using one teacher with three classes and several teacher aides. The supply of teachers is going to get worse before it gets better."

— A Director of Instructional Materials

"We've got to have conscientious, dedicated, determined Negro teachers who are willing to 'let blood for their own people.' We should emphasize really gutsy instruction in Negro schools. Negro teachers tend to be stern, while white teachers are permissive. The important thing is that instruction happens in the classroom or it doesn't."

— A Superintendent

"Usually four teachers here combine their classes to watch TV on alternate dates, so that two of us can get coffee breaks."

— A Teacher

(3) **Interfering environmental realities**

"This past year I had every piece of audio-visual equipment — over $4,000 worth — stolen."

— A Principal

"Make curriculum relevant? I don't care what we have to do to motivate these kids. Once we do, it would be wrong for them to get any idea they can survive in our competitive society without learning to speak and read English, and enough about numbers to earn a living."

— A Deputy Superintendent

"The words I hear most often are 'What's the use?' The majority of my children have become self-defeating. They are lethargic about education. They love to be entertained and to socialize, but not to work. They don't see any point in working. Their goals are too fleeting and too temporary."

— A Principal

"The caste system in the Negro community is much more rigid than in any white community. In poverty schools, most teachers are Negro. Negro teachers live in Richmond Heights with their swimming pools. There is an alienation between the ghetto and these 'wetbacks'."

— A Superintendent

"The language poverty of our children is terrific. Parents do not have time to talk to their children, or just don't talk to them. The conditions in our schools keep teachers from having enough opportunity to talk individually to the children."

— A Supervisor

"I checked a third grade class last week. Only four pupils had started in that same school. The average child had moved at least five times."

— A Principal

"Last year I had one third grade boy who had been in and out of 28 schools in his first three years."

— A Supervisor

"In many schools we have 125% change-over of pupils within one year. These include the gifted and the disadvantaged, made up of those newly arrived from the South and the non-English-speaking who are largely Puerto Rican. The great challenge is meeting the language and dialect difficulties of these 'youngsters on wheels'."

— An Assistant Superintendent

"Every day all the teachers in my school are six-hour immigrants into the Watts area."

— A Principal

(4) Administrative leadership and practices

"Some principals simply reject new programs out-of-hand. They are too set in old ways and refuse to recognize such a problem as the basic need for compensatory enrichment programs."

— A Director of Special Programs

"Before we made a systematic upgrading effort, the Negro high school diploma meant virtually nothing. It was a phony. Now the kids are at least going to know how to read, write, spell and figure."

— A Superintendent

"If the administration feels a particular television source is important for a particular group of the pupil population, then it should recommend or require that it be used regularly in the classrooms for which it was designed."

— A Teacher

"Half the audio-visual materials ordered are not practical for the particular subjects or units being taught. Materials are only available months in advance. The logistics program in audio-visual materials here is antique."

— A Teacher

"Buying instructional materials is done from the top down. The administration wastes a lot of money buying equipment teachers do not want. Everyone in this school has a record player, but there are no records available."

— A Teacher

"We would prefer to use audio-visual materials over television, but get discouraged. We have to order the films so far in advance. A few of our requests are confirmed and acted upon when we need them."

— A Teacher

"The purchasing department at City Hall buys any item over $50. We need to allow a year to a year-and-a-half for planning and getting materials. Even when money is available for an item, we expect to wait at least five months in processing the purchase order. On films, we wait only two and one-half months."

— A Director of Instructional Materials

"It's like trying to fix a bicycle while you're riding on it."

— A Superintendent

(5) Communication between administrators, teachers, parents, community, and children

"The adequacy of communications, both to the staff and the community, is one of our biggest problems. The state and federal forces are often stronger than our local ones, which are marked by inaction and disinterest. The local teachers' organizations are also pushing for control and this, too, frustrates our communications with the staff. The only place in town where we could assemble all the faculty is in the ball park. In fact, we tried this ten years ago. Now I've been talking to the staff over television."

— A Superintendent

"So few parents really know what the score is in the schools."

— A School Board Member

"You must bring the community along with you. One of the great advantages of adult education is that if the adults in the community benefit personally, they will be much stronger supporters of TV for their kids."

— A Superintendent

"One acute problem is the lack of administrators' and teachers' sensitivity. Surely there are more ways to communicate than those using proper Ann Arbor English."

— A School Board Member

"Television should be used much more for administrative use. Here we have a mass medium which, more than any other we know about, is a more personal way for the Superintendent to get across to his staff what he wants."

— An Assistant Superintendent

"The public sees technology as a frill . . . our teachers are constantly trying to use more audio-visual equipment. If the budget would allow it, they would be using much more. Some teachers have even bought their own overhead projectors."

— A Principal

(6) Excessive load on teachers

"Some teachers use television well, and really want more of it. Teachers are not reluctant to use it if it is convenient, available, and relevant."

— A Supervisor

"We want materials that are accessible, available and **simple**."

— A Teacher

(7) Insufficient and/or unpredictable financial support

"If we do begin television with our own facilities here, it must not be on a shoestring. If that is the case, that is where it will stay."

— A Deputy Superintendent

"Several of our severe problems stem from the unreliability of foundation and federal support — that is, the threat of cancellation. For example, we have geared up with staff and schools for a team teaching project with Ford Foundation and ESEA Title III, and now there is a threat of cut-back."

— An Associate Director of Instruction

"There is the whole problem of paying the teachers of teachers. Our principals and experienced teachers now give in-service training after school as volunteers on their own time. The colleges who hire our staff experts pay them. Why shouldn't the public schools?"

— An Associate Director of Instruction

"We spend 96% of our budget on salaries."

— A Superintendent

"The teacher gets to take home 50¢ per day per child. That is very cheap babysitting."

— A Principal

(8) Inadequate facilities

"We use the cafeteria for large-group instruction. The kids eat out-of-doors. We need to change the tables three times a day. Moving the tables in and out almost makes it not worth it."

— A Principal

"We have one set in our school. We can't get it moved around the building fast enough to start at the beginning of programs. If the teacher using the set earlier is on another floor, there isn't time enough to move the set. We need one set per room. A busy teacher suddenly looks up. It is 10:45, too late to get the set, move it into the room, get it warmed up, tune it in properly, and prepare the students for the program. The reception is often poor too. With such pressures, teachers feel it is not worth the effort for using even the best TV program."

— A Principal

"We need TV with headsets, so that small groups of pupils can listen to it."

— A Teacher

"Our TV sets are generally in the auditoriums. This really only works in the classroom situation."

— A Supervisor

"There are so few television sets in most buildings that teachers don't even think about using the programs. Until there is at least one set per two teachers, and preferably one per classroom, teachers will stick to their original lesson plans and not bother with television."

— A Principal

II CURRENT STATUS OF SCHOOL TELEVISION IN THE GREAT CITIES

(1) Descriptive comments

"It is marvelous how TV can mesmerize and hold the attention of a group of kids and teachers. Whether it is teaching anything or not is another story."

— A Principal

"When I visit schools, I find little utilization. When I ask for statistics on the use of TV, they seem to be too positive."

— An Assistant Superintendent

"More teachers are using commercial stations than they do the educational stations."

— A Principal

"Our TV is much better than it was before. We're doing fewer live programs, using higher quality programs produced elsewhere, or nationally by the National Center for School and College Television, Eastern Educational Network, and MPATI. We are spending more dollars per program. We're becoming more critical because more is available and we can be more selective. But we should spend even more dollars and time on each program, and search harder for better talent."

— An Associate Director, Elementary Instruction

"When our programs came over commercial stations, we had much better quality and reception than now. But it's improving."
— A Supervisor

"Our evaluation is pretty subjective. We have a teacher committee that evaluates each program produced. This can be very critical or constructive."
— A Director of Instruction

"When the program is relevant and important to the instructional program, the youngsters look forward to following it just as though it was a series on commercial television."
— A Teacher

"We bring programs to children, but they are in reality a great benefit to the teacher."
— A Curriculum Specialist

"The elementary teacher is a generalist. These teachers know what they don't know and are more receptive. One teacher is with the youngsters all day. The schedule is much more manipulatable. At the secondary and junior college levels, everything is broken down by subject area and the scheduling is simply impossible with the one open-circuit broadcast setup we how have."
— An Assistant Superintendent

"The brighter, more creative child gets the most out of instructional television, particularly if there is a provocative and interesting program."
— A Teacher

"The kind of programs needed for inner-city youngsters are not the same as the general materials we are now getting through the community television station. This one-channel service for the entire metropolitan area is not really adequate for our needs."
— A Deputy Superintendent

"Television here hasn't done anything but supplement the traditional. The potential is certainly there. But we haven't spent time or money to think about it, play with it, promote it. The trouble is that the TV people seem to be so busy with the engineering, hardware, and empire building that they are really not using its creative potential. So far, they have just been very successful in making it bland."
— A Superintendent

"If audio-visual materials were available in abundance, they could do everything that TV can do, and do it better and more flexibly."
— A Deputy Superintendent

"We either ought to get television in as a significant part of the educational program, or let's get out of it altogether."
— A Supervisor

"Improved use of television can only come from top-level sympathy plus a commitment to the value that hasn't really been explored. We need **talent** for leadership. The educational television station isn't concerned with the problems of the inner city; its main concern is with the suburban community."
— A Deputy Superintendent

"The program quality here is low because programs are written and produced by teachers. They are not professionals in this area."
— A Deputy Superintendent

"There's nothing on instructional television for the kids now. We used to have a ninth grade English program. It was a total flop. We discontinued it. We are asking for in-service teacher training to introduce new English, reaching into it all at once — the new grammar, semantics, and linguistics."

— A Director of English

"Radio is doing more for the teacher than television here in St. Louis."

— A Teacher

"We should raise to a higher level in the school organization the structure that deals with television. Television is too far removed from top management contact."

— A Superintendent

"Television has not done a helluva lot for Buffalo."

— An Administrator

(2) School Television: highlights and promising practices

"Last year we found ourselves trying to pass a $189½ million bond issue. We had lost the previous one, when we used very little television, and we weren't going to lose this one. With enormous support by television, the result was 73.2% in our favor."

— A Superintendent

"Those who say that deprived children cannot learn should see our inner-city students learning foreign languages. There's a prestige factor here. They're proud to be taking French or Spanish, like the kids in the suburbs do. The teachers complain that the televised programs go too fast, but the pupils don't find them a bit too rapid."

— A Director of Educational Radio & TV

"Administrative uses? We're now broadcasting Board meetings at 9:30 p.m. There are several programs geared to parents, such as on the new report card, and inviting the parents' help on Reading."

— An Associate Superintendent

"The most successful use of television here has been the Superintendent's presentation of the Board Report. It was a high-quality program. The teachers of the community enjoy getting the information at the same time."

— A Supervisor

"The most successful uses of television for the youngsters are not during the school day. Teachers assign outside viewing as they would outside reading — like the Young People's Concert of the New York Philharmonic on Saturday morning."

— A Director of Secondary Education

"TV beamed into school is great in overcoming the decline of teachers' institutes (as mandated by the unions), meeting needs in areas where teachers feel insecure, like the New Math, Linguistics, mass media, and Social Studies."

— A Director of Secondary Education

"The lack of communication in a system as large as ours and a lack of knowledge of what is going on are tremendous. The teachers simply don't know. The teachers' organizations are worse. Use of television by the Superintendent helps to give true, living perspective. He not only tells them what the policies are, but also conveys who is ultimately responsible for them. Bulletins are not enough. Closed-circuit television would help a great deal in getting much more of this."

— An Associate Superintendent

"Our East Technical High School is in deep trouble. In the homes of these kids, the toilets won't work, violence is the rule, and fires are frequent. Twenty homes have been burnt recently and stand as empty shells. The community is a total failure, except for the high school's winning basketball team. It beats all the teams in the State except one, going all the way to the State championship.

"The morale in the community was positive for the first time. The State championship game was played at a small college over ETV. To tune into this game, broadcast over a UHF channel, a special converter had to be added to the regular VHF sets. The people from this community cleaned out all of the stores all over town to get these converters. This may perhaps be more important in evaluating the impact of television than trying to measure certain instructional refinements."

— A Superintendent

(3) School Television: constraints and deterrents

"Scheduling and time are deterrent factors — especially in the high schools. The teacher's attitude too often is that 'I can't take time from my "regular" program.' If our schools could have their own station and channels they would be great assets for teacher training. For example, we would introduce the new math and other new curricula to teachers much more systematically."

— An Associate Director, Elementary Instruction

"Why not put instructional films into the school and compare results the with TV in the closed-circuit high school we have? What we need is a candid study of alternatives."

— A Deputy Superintendent

"We must have people who really know how to make **top quality programs**. This might take half of the experienced television people."

— An Assistant Superintendent

"When the novelty wears off, will television still grab them? Will kids really continue to concentrate or will they sleep, curl hair, and glance at the boyfriend?"

— A School Board Member

"We need a candid appraisal of television, analyzing its potentials and limitations, rather than any selling of a bill of goods. We need to know what it can and cannot do."

— A Deputy Superintendent

"Television programs take kids out of the ghetto. Educational television must learn to do this better. It is not being used to help teach skills, providing motivation and interest so that individual instruction can be more effective."

— A Principal

"The conditions for viewing instructional television are terrible. We must start improving them at the classroom level. And fancy facilities are not necessarily the answer."

— A Community ETV Station School Specialist

"The quality of outside sources of televised courses — such as Great Plains or the Center at Indiana University — is not adequate or in line with our system's needs. When programs go into these national libraries they are, on the average, three years old and get dated too quickly."

— A Superintendent

"I would like to see educators given some training in performance over television, and the TV people better grounded in education. We need more professionalism all the way around. This also applies to the preparation of teachers' guides."

— A School Board Member

"The teaching of Spanish to 400 — 500 in an auditorium is just what we don't want. Kids must have individual attention. There's no substitute for this."

— An Assistant Superintendent

"We haven't had sufficient evaluation to know what works (both the medium itself and the specific programs) and what doesn't. Until then, we won't put out $3 million for CCTV cables. We have to be sure that the money would be better spent on this than on books or teachers' salaries. Can you really teach American History and Institutions, with a visit to the Supreme Court, having a national government course used by all cities, leaving room for local government programs?"

— A School Board Member

"Our television productions are now too often 'show' rather than sound education and instruction. We must tie the programs into the **regular curriculum.** It is very hard to get TV people really to tie in and get assistance and direction from the people running our educational program. This is not only here; when I visited Hagerstown the television and curriculum people couldn't even meet with each other. There was absolutely no communication."

— An Associate Superintendent

"Without acceptance from teachers, television is like turning the pages of a book that the teacher hasn't even read."

— A Superintendent

"There's a fundamental inflexibility of MPATI, treating all the kids in a five-state area the same way. It's bad enough to assume this in one classroom."

— A Superintendent

"I won't be satisfied with evaluation results unless the teachers and administrators are happy. Does the staff which uses it feel that it helps them do a more effective job?"

— A Superintendent

"It is sad when the supervisors have to open up our radio and TV bulletin to find out what's going on."

— An Assistant Superintendent

"Participation is difficult over TV. The key problem is lack of interaction in all educational technology, between the teachers and the youngsters, and among the youngsters. Technology is especially good for drill."

— A Deputy Superintendent

"There is an awful lot of good material not being used on ITV. We must work out this problem with copyright laws. Now, we just don't use much film or other valuable materials that we would like to. How can we simplify this? The clearance problems have got to be worked out. You can see the conflict between using one film over TV versus thirty or forty copies for audio-visual use. What's the practical compromise here, fair to both sides? We can't even buy network footage from CBS and NBC because there are no provisions for schools to buy a good documentary film. The networks occasionally _give_ us material but they won't sell. Not using excellent materials is wasteful."

— An Associate Superintendent

"We need a TV coordinator in each school building who is not some guy getting stuck with the job."

— An ETV Station Manager

"The programs are not provocative enough. Educators make TV duller than the teacher in the classroom. If it is to be successful, it must be exciting and different, well organized, and superbly presented."

— A Supervisor

"The quality of programs is good. But they are not often what my pupils need. I would like to have a greater quantity to choose from."

— A Principal

"Sets are not repaired when they are broken or replaced when they are stolen."

— A Supervisor

"No one cares if you use TV here or not."

— A Supervisor

"Many of our teachers have been looking forward to TV to augment their teaching. But they know of many teachers in other schools who have rejected it as something which is inconvenient, irrelevant, and unimportant to the program."

— A Principal

"The biggest complaint about television is that teachers are unable to see it before it is played over the air. That makes it difficult to use."

— A Principal

"The television station here is trying to serve too many audiences with no responsibility to any one of them."

— A Supervisor

". . . put two or three programs on that flop, and the sets go dead."

— A Director of Instruction

"We would like to use programs, if they were abundant enough to have special groups of children viewing them on their own. But then the programs would have to be designed specifically for certain target audiences — not for every child taking fourth-grade Mathematics but for those, let's say, having trouble with sets in New Math, or sentence construction in English."

— A Teacher

"When TV lessons are supposed to use certain coordinated materials, our experience is that only one out of thirty of the things needed is available at the time the program is broadcast. They are just not available to everybody. This is something the school system should look into."

— A Teacher

"Instructional television came in here at a high administrative level. That set up a negative reaction from the teachers. Classroom development was needed which did not take place. Now it seems to be more a part of the classroom teacher's thinking."

— A Director of Audio-Visual Education

"There is too much use of the same series year after year. The result is that the freshness has left."

— A Director of Community Relations

"I should know more about instructional television than I do. It's a serious personal shortcoming."

— A Superintendent

"If we go to TV in (high school) Math, it will be a last resort to support the unqualified teacher."

— A Curriculum Specialist

"TV programs tend to do too much that can be done in class. They should concentrate on areas not easily handled in the classroom, such as for poor readers and those who do not have the fundamentals to build on."

— A Principal

"There is a star system among TV teachers."

— **A Community ETV Station Director**

"Until television actually teaches core information about a subject, and does it well enough to replace the teacher in some of her work, it will never really pay off."

— **A Supervisor**

"I have high hopes for television and would like to cooperate in helping to realize them. We don't have enough channels, however, and the quality of both programs and reception is poor. The school system had better decide whether quality ITV programs are desired or, it should give television up as a bad job."

— **A Curriculum Specialist**

"The word **voluntary** kills us all. We need less voluntary support and more leadership."

— **An ETV Station Manager**

"Generally, the programming has been ancillary and fragmentary. There has been much 'entertainment' unrelated to the tough 'thinking' job the teacher has to do. There are also the mechanical and logistical problems of reception, maintenance, scheduling, and the pilfering of TV sets from the schools. They are stealing us blind."

— **A Superintendent**

"Any administrative program has to be awfully good if it is to be effective. When you put on a television program and are reaching 3,000 teachers and sometimes 72,000 children, you must give it the best possible program preparation."

— **An Associate Superintendent**

"TV here is just amateur night in the daytime."

— **A Teacher**

"There is now no use of television for credit courses toward professional advancement, unless the teachers are enrolled directly in a college program in which television is used. There is no coordination between the schools and the colleges on this. We could suggest it to the colleges, or vice versa."

— **A Superintendent**

(4) Directions of development, and potentials

"How about using instructional television for gifted kids to communicate across the city? . . . As for computers, there is very little creativity here; this is mainly a record-keeping function. In fact, they merely seem to be automating record-keeping as it was done in the old way. It is often the same with television: teachers teaching the same class in the same way, only projected over television — even with excellent teachers."

— **A Superintendent**

"Big cities waste a lot of time in duplicated efforts. A basic course in American History or a good film on the teaching of Newton's Laws can be as good in New York City as it is in Chicago. The same principle applies in reaching the parents. We should pool efforts for program development and share expenses. Why start all over again in every area?"

— **A Superintendent**

"Greater commitment is required. This can be achieved by involving our best people in it, especially in developing the programs. We should: (1) spend as much time and effort in developing quality instructional television programs as they do on commercial television; (2) make it an integral part of our curriculum rather than something 'nice to have around' if we're really going to increase utilization; and (3) prepare teachers for using television as well as we try to prepare them to use their new textbooks."

— **A Superintendent**

"There is a commonality about needs in the big cities. We should see to it that programs are so real, and so much at the heart of this problem in our country, that we could not help but use them and integrate them into our curriculum."

— A Superintendent

"Television can be a tremendous adjunct to the teacher if you have the right kind of materials to meet individual differences. It helps to see things in another form."

— A Superintendent

"There is a tremendous potential for television in teacher education. We could do a great deal better in insuring completeness, accuracy, and enthusiasm through the common experience of TV. The union and teachers' organizations are going to insist on credit. Their present argument is that teachers should be paid to attend as well as earn credits for their salary increment. In any event, we've got to back up the teachers more effectively."

— An Assistant Superintendent

"Why not use television for attendance reports instead of involving teachers in hours of clerical work? Why use horse-and-buggy procedures when trying to serve 600 separate sites involving over 50,000 people on the payroll?"

— An Administrator

"All changes in education tend to be somewhat glacial. The icy part is the teacher who puts in a minimal amount of time on his own advancement. If learning comes primarily from human interaction, then we must find ways of *upgrading teachers first*. We desperately need a linkage between television and the total educational program, including materials, activities, and what goes on in the classroom. While TV is just another resource, the thing that excites me about it is its flexibility. Think of bringing TV into the schools, particularly the secondary classes, by taping during the night for subsequent replay during the day."

— A Superintendent

"It would be great to have a program for teachers once a month on new methods and materials — and especially good if we got teachers involved in the program. Another way would be to have a teachers' meeting every two weeks, run twice a day, at noon and after school."

— A Supervisor

"We had better develop visual teaching materials with the same care and expertise being used to develop commercials for television, using techniques that persuade."

— A Supervisor

"One real potential is for canning lessons for students not present, especially demonstrations."

— A Director of Curriculum

"We would like to see resource packages on broad subjects like the Western States. These could consist of film clips, lesson plans, follow-up suggestions, and guide sheets. They could be flexible, changing specific components of the kit rather than having to re-do an entire tape or series due to obsolescence."

— A Supervisor

"Whenever a program has an instructor with a dynamic personality, it succeeds. Poor personality results in no appeal. It won't work. We ought to develop a star system of teachers who can be heroes to children."

— A Deputy Superintendent

"A good classroom teacher is as good as any TV teacher, but TV can bring a whole rich world of reality to the classroom. No teacher can do that."

— A Deputy Superintendent

"How about using television for making teachers more aware of the variety of instructional materials available and the diversity of their use?"

— A Director of Instructional Materials

"We have to quit looking at TV as just a pig-in-a-poke. We often try to sell things on a city-wide basis when we should be paying closer attention to what particular schools need. Let's take one school at a time, and develop an R&D program."

— An Assistant Superintendent

"Children get enough of adults talking to them. Why can't they develop programs that involve children of approximately the same age? The main purpose of television is to motivate children, and to broaden their horizons and vision."

— A Teacher

"I feel that ITV will be forced to go into color, as it becomes widely adopted by public broadcast television."

— A Superintendent

"The key question is, 'Do you do basic stuff the teachers want and need, or is it "fringe" stuff?' It made a basic contribution when the State required a course on the State constitution. Few teachers knew much about it. Even fewer were interested in teaching it. TV did it. No one wants to teach Gonorrhea; let TV do it and we'd say 'Thank God for ETV'."

— A Superintendent

III. ON COOPERATION AMONG GREAT CITIES

"It always helps in getting funds for a program if there is a community of interest and we can say 'It's been done successfully elsewhere.' Evidence of a successful practice can sway local authorities. And vice versa, something that has not been successful should not be tried here."

— A Superintendent

"I'd like to see television used for better and faster communication among cities. Why not dream a little about a nationwide hook-up for intercommunication, including program exchange? This would simplify previewing programs."

— A Superintendent

"Television is still feeling its way. I can remember educational radio. We grabbed onto that new medium as the answer to our problems. Then we went through a period of discouragement. Now we must move ahead in a more mature, balanced fashion. We need people who don't see television as a panacea or as a threat. We need those who are thinking in terms of what steps must be taken to make it effective. We are not going to do this through books or dissertations. We need a plan of action developed by those who realistically understand the needs of big-city school systems. Creative practitioners are more likely to be of help to us than university professors who don't understand our problems."

— An Assistant Superintendent

"The Great Cities together are like a bundle of twigs. They have a great deal more financial capability."

— A Superintendent

"Through coordinated planning and production, we could get much more choice and greater quality. But the key issue is, which cities are to work in which areas?"

— A Superintendent

"We need some on-going relationship between the cities to facilitate exchanges and joint programming. There is no sense in having each school system invent the wheel each time it needs one."

— A Superintendent

"We have done well through the Research Council in bringing together job-alike people in the big-city school systems for textbook adoption procedures, pioneering practices in teacher education, and vocational education. In short, getting together people with similar problems and goals is useful. They meet, plan, develop policy guidelines, and work together on joint programs."
— An Associate Superintendent

"Don't tell me that the ghetto problem in Detroit isn't the same as the ghetto problem in New York."
— A Superintendent

"Why is it that a good film on Newton's Laws isn't as good in Chicago as it is in New York. Are the principles of Physics any different there?"
— A Superintendent

"If the Great Cities Research Council Instructional Materials Committee clearly goes on record that a school district should own its own station, this would provide valuable back-up support for the Board in selling to the community the need of our doing so."
— An Associate Superintendent

APPENDIX C

CHARTS ON INSTRUCTIONAL PROBLEMS

The question, "What are the most acute instructional problems facing your school system today?" was the lead question asked in 218 separate interviews involving 393 people in the 16 Great Cities. This free response question was answered by 17 Superintendents and Board Members, 70 School Administrators, 102 Curriculum Supervisors, 70 Principals, 101 Teachers, and 33 Instructional Materials and Television personnel.

The objectives of the question were to appraise: (1) if the instructional problems expressed by this cross-section of professional educators were consistent with the needs instructional television was serving; (2) if the different professional groups expressed general agreement on their most acute instructional problems; (3) if all cities expressed general agreement as to their most acute instructional problems; and (4) to begin the interview by encouraging each person to talk about those problems he feels are most important.

The method and time permitted interviews in breadth but in little depth. The persons interviewed were generally selected by an administrator assigned by the Superintendent of Schools to work with the researchers. Therefore, the interviews were not a random sample, not of equal number in each city, nor of equal number or proportion from the different professional groups.

After a thorough review of the responses to this open-ended question, it was determined that all answers could be placed in eight broad categories. In ranked order these broad problem areas were: (1) curriculum relevance, diversity and resources; (2) teacher quality and quantity; (3) interfering environmental realities; (4) teacher workload; (5) internal and external communications; (6) administrative leadership and practices; (7) insufficient and/or unpredictable financial support; and (8) inadequate or obsolete facilities. Often during an interview two or more answers could relate to one of the eight broad problem areas. This related group of answers would be counted as only one response when assigned to a broad problem area. There was an average ratio of almost three specific answers to one assigned response. The first four charts of Appendix C are based on the 543 responses. The last four charts are based on the tabulation of all the specific answers given in the interviews to the four highest ranked problem areas (Curriculum, Teachers, Environment, and Workload). The answers have been grouped under descriptive sub-categories for convenience of interpretation.

TABLE H

NUMBER OF INTERVIEWS USING QUESTIONNAIRES

	Supt. & 3 Bd. Mem.	Administrators	Supervisors	IM & TV Personnel	Principals	Teachers	SUB-TOTAL	Other Persons Interviewed	TOTAL Persons Interviewed
Baltimore	0/0	4/4	3/9	1/1	3/9	3/9	14/32	8	40
Boston	1/1	2/4	1/1	0/0	2/2	1/1	7/9	9	18
Buffalo	1/1	4/4	1/2	1/1	1/1	0/0	8/9	2	11
Chicago	1/1	2/2	1/2	2/2	2/6	1/9	9/22	2	24
Cleveland	1/1	2/2	4/9	2/2	3/7	7/3	19/24	4	28
Detroit	1/1	3/3	3/4	1/2	1/1	2/4	11/15	3	18
Los Angeles	2/2	8/9	5/9	4/4	2/3	2/9	23/36	7	43
Memphis	1/1	1/1	3/8	0/0	2/6	2/6	9/22	3	25
Milwaukee	1/1	2/2	4/10	1/1	3/4	4/7	15/25	4	29
New York	1/1	10/12	4/4	1/3	0/0	1/4	17/24	2	26
Philadelphia	1/1	6/7	4/11	1/1	2/4	1/3	15/27	12	39
Pittsburgh	1/1	6/6	4/11	4/4	1/3	3/15	19/40	4	44
St. Louis	2/2	2/5	4/10	2/2	3/8	2/6	15/33	5	38
San Diego	1/1	3/3	3/7	3/4	2/6	3/10	15/31	5	36
San Francisco	1/1	4/4	1/3	3/3	3/10	3/11	15/32	5	37
Washington D.C.	1/1	2/2	2/2	2/3	0/0	0/0	7/8	2	10
	17/17	61/70	47/102	28/33	30/70	35/101	218/389	77	466

KEY: Number of Interviews/Number of Persons Interviewed (Questionnaire #1)

THE CITIES' MOST ACUTE INSTRUCTIONAL PROBLEMS

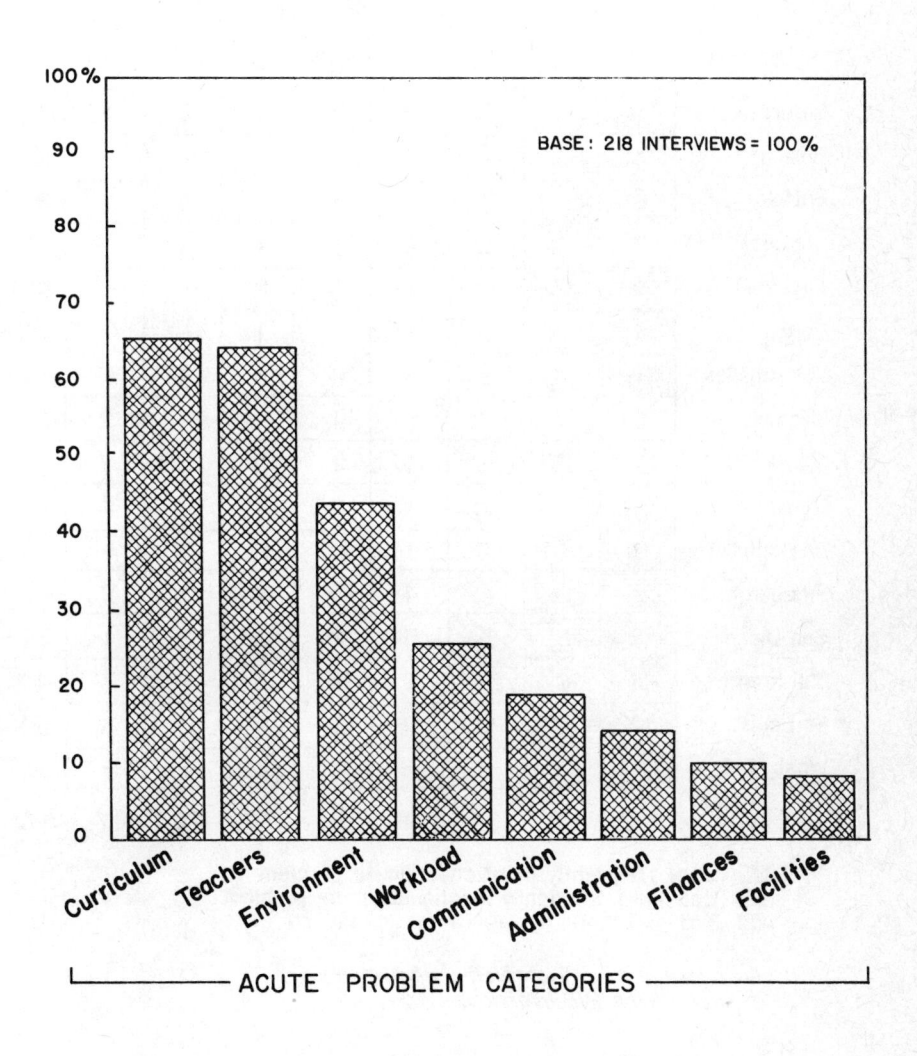

Figure 1

MOST ACUTE INSTRUCTIONAL PROBLEMS
(BY CITIES)

	CURRICULUM	TEACHERS	ENVIRONMENT	WORKLOAD	COMMUNICATION	ADMINISTRATION	FINANCES	FACILITIES	
Baltimore	10	9	6	3	2	3	2	1	36
Boston	4	5	6	3	1	2	–	–	21
Buffalo	6	8	3	–	1	1	4	1	24
Chicago	3	6	6	4	1	1	1	–	22
Cleveland	8	13	13	7	6	2	–	–	45
Detroit	9	7	2	2	–	1	–	1	22
Los Angeles	16	14	8	6	8	3	4	–	54
Memphis	2	7	7	5	1	–	1	2	24
Milwaukee	7	10	6	6	1	2	2	2	36
New York	13	11	10	1	3	1	–	–	39
Philadelphia	11	9	2	1	4	2	–	–	30
Pittsburgh	11	14	6	4	5	4	1	2	47
San Diego	12	6	5	3	2	3	2	1	34
San Francisco	12	6	9	2	4	3	1	3	40
St. Louis	12	13	10	4	1	–	2	3	50
Wash. D.C.	6	3	–	–	2	2	1	–	14
No. of Responses	142	141	94	56	41	30	22	17	543

- ▦ Most frequently mentioned acute problem
- ▤ 2nd most frequently mentioned acute problem
- ▨ 3rd   "   "   "   "   "   "

An average of 2.5 problems were mentioned in each of the 218 interviews

Figure 2

THE MOST ACUTE INSTRUCTIONAL PROBLEMS

AS SEEN BY PERSONS WITH DIFFERENT PROFESSIONAL RESPONSIBILITIES

AREAS OF CONCERN	PROFESSIONAL GROUPS: SUPERINTENDENTS & BOARD MEMBERS	ADMINISTRATORS	SUPERVISORS	PRINCIPALS	TEACHERS	INST. MATERIAL & TV PERSONNEL	
Curriculum	14	55	26	16	16	14	142
Teachers	9	39	34	22	24	13	141
Environment	4	27	21	15	21	6	94
Workload	1	2	14	15	23	1	56
Communication	2	12	12	4	9	2	41
Administration	–	7	2	5	9	7	30
Finances	4	7	4	2	1	4	21
Facilities	1	4	4	4	4	–	17
No. of Responses out of 218 Interviews	35	153	117	83	107	47	***543***

Most frequently mentioned acute problem

2nd most frequently mentioned acute problem

3rd " " " " " " " " " "

Figure 3

PERCENTAGE OF INTERVIEW RESPONSES ON THE ACUTE INSTRUCTIONAL PROBLEMS
BY PERSONS WITH DIFFERING PROFESSIONAL RESPONSIBILITIES

	CURRICULUM	TEACHERS	WORKLOAD OF TEACHERS	ENVIRONMENT	% of Total No. of Responses in Each Grouping*
Superintendents	40%	26%	3%	11%	80%
Administrators	36%	28%	1%	17%	82%
Supervisors	22%	29%	12%	17%	80%
Principals	19%	27%	17%	18%	81%
Teachers	15%	22%	21%	20%	78%
Inst. Material & TV Personnel	30%	28%	2%	13%	73%

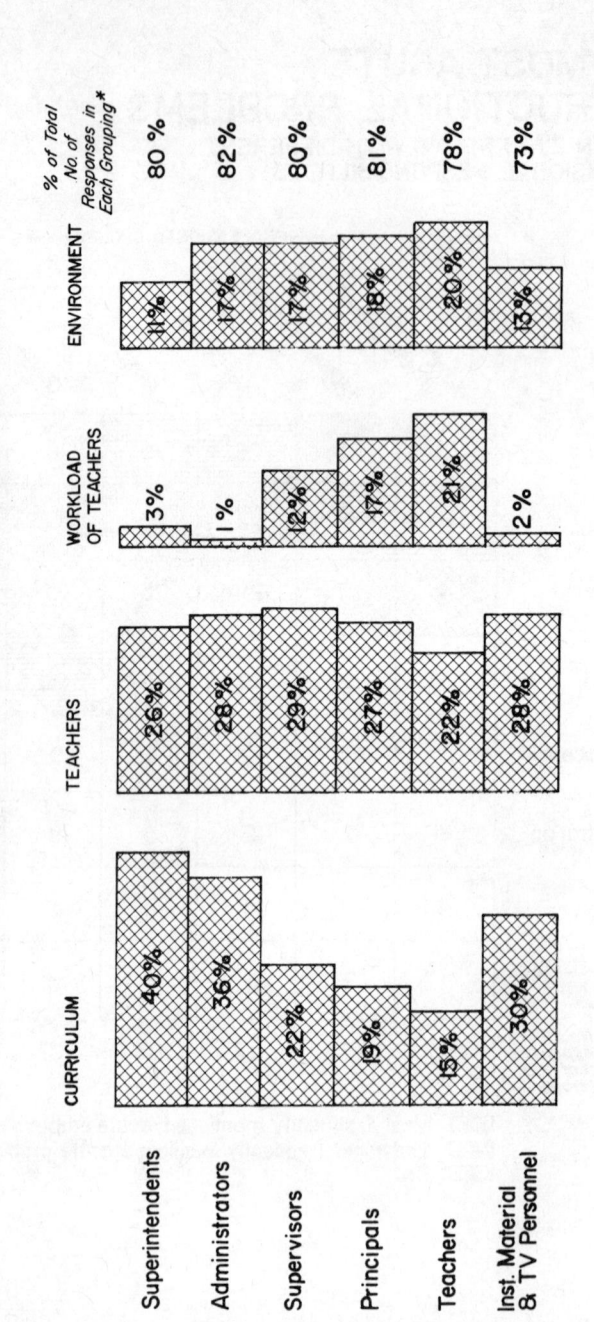

* The remaining percentage of responses were in the areas of Communication, Administration, Finances and Facilities.

Figure 13

CURRICULUM INADEQUACIES

	RELEVANCE OF PROGRAM (for meeting today's requirements)	DIVERSITY OF PROGRAM (for meeting individual needs toward achievement)	APPROPRIATE INSTRUCTIONAL MATERIALS & EQUIPMENT	DEVELOPMENT OF LANGUAGE & COMPUTATION SKILLS	NEED EVALUATION & PUPIL ASSESSMENT TOOLS & PROCEDURES	
Baltimore	▓	▓				15
Boston	▓					9
Buffalo	▓	▓				13
Chicago			▓			5
Cleveland			▓			10
Detroit	▓					17
Los Angeles	▓		▓			24
Memphis						4
Milwaukee	▓	▓				13
New York	▓			▓		24
Philadelphia		▓				17
Pittsburgh		▓				19
San Diego	▓					23
San Francisco	▓					21
St. Louis			▓			18
Wash. D.C.			▓			14
No. of Responses	77	65	56	35	13	*246*

▓ 25% or more of a city's responses concerning curriculum inadequacies

Figure 14

TEACHER NEEDS

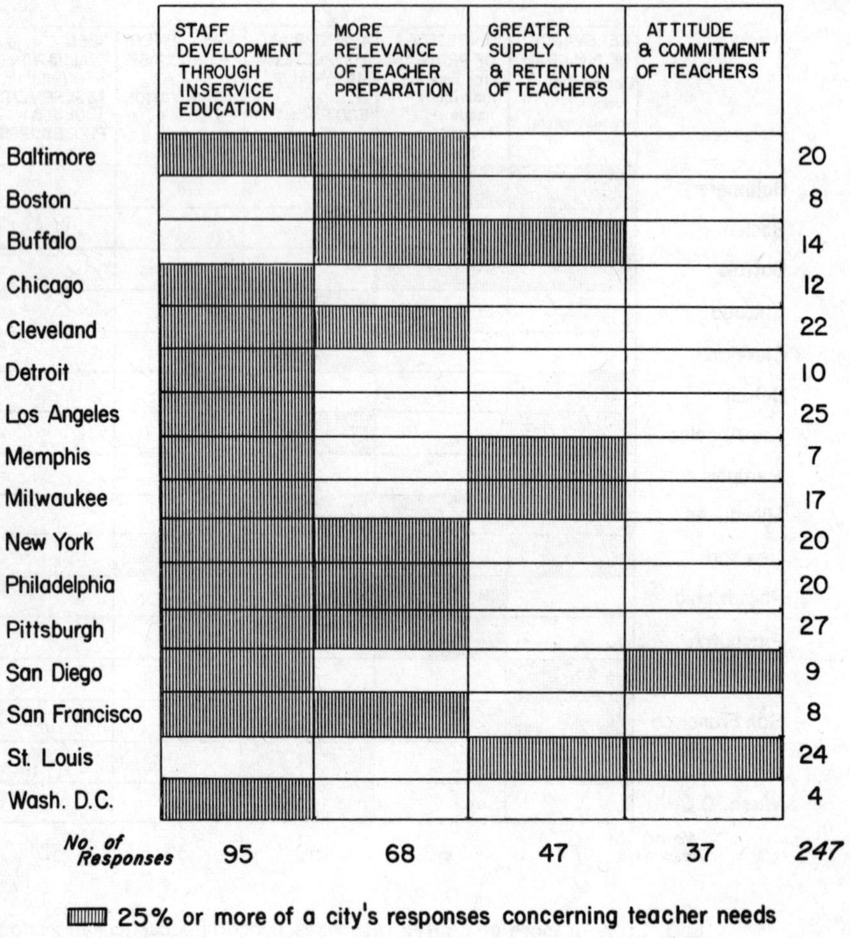

	STAFF DEVELOPMENT THROUGH INSERVICE EDUCATION	MORE RELEVANCE OF TEACHER PREPARATION	GREATER SUPPLY & RETENTION OF TEACHERS	ATTITUDE & COMMITMENT OF TEACHERS	
Baltimore	▓	▓			20
Boston		▓			8
Buffalo		▓	▓		14
Chicago	▓				12
Cleveland		▓			22
Detroit	▓				10
Los Angeles					25
Memphis	▓		▓		7
Milwaukee	▓				17
New York	▓	▓			20
Philadelphia	▓	▓			20
Pittsburgh	▓	▓			27
San Diego	▓			▓	9
San Francisco	▓				8
St. Louis			▓	▓	24
Wash. D.C.	▓				4
No. of Responses	95	68	47	37	247

▓ 25% or more of a city's responses concerning teacher needs

Figure 15

INTERFERING ENVIRONMENTAL REALITIES

	LANGUAGE DEFICIENCIES (Non-English, Dialect & Retardation)	EXPERIENCE & PHYSICAL DEPRIVATION	MOTIVATION & ASPIRATION OF PUPILS	MOBILITY OF PUPILS & FAMILIES	PSYCHOLOGICAL & SOCIAL ADJUSTMENT	
Baltimore		▓	▓		▓	12
Boston			▓			11
Buffalo		▓				4
Chicago	▓	▓	▓			15
Cleveland		▓	▓		▓	12
Detroit		▓				4
Los Angeles		▓				13
Memphis	▓			▓		11
Milwaukee			▓		▓	11
New York	▓					17
Philadelphia		▓				3
Pittsburgh	▓		▓			14
San Diego				▓		13
San Francisco	▓					13
St. Louis			▓	▓		23
Wash. D.C.						0
No. of Responses	44	43	40	32	18	*177*

▓▓▓ 25% or more of a cities responses concerning environmental problems

Figure 16

EXCESSIVE WORKLOAD OF TEACHERS

City	FEWER PUPILS PER TEACHER	RELIEF TIME FOR TEACHERS TO PLAN AND WORK WITH INDIVIDUALS	MORE SPECIAL TEACHERS	No. of Responses
Baltimore	▓▓▓	▓▓▓		8
Boston		▓▓▓		3
Buffalo				—
Chicago	▓▓▓			4
Cleveland	▓▓▓			8
Detroit	▓▓▓			2
Los Angeles		▓▓▓		8
Memphis	▓▓▓	▓▓▓		11
Milwaukee	▓▓▓			8
New York				1
Philadelphia		▓▓▓		1
Pittsburgh	▓▓▓	▓▓▓		7
San Diego	▓▓▓	▓▓▓		6
San Francisco				3
St. Louis	▓▓▓			10
Washington D.C.				—

No. of Responses: 40   30   10   80

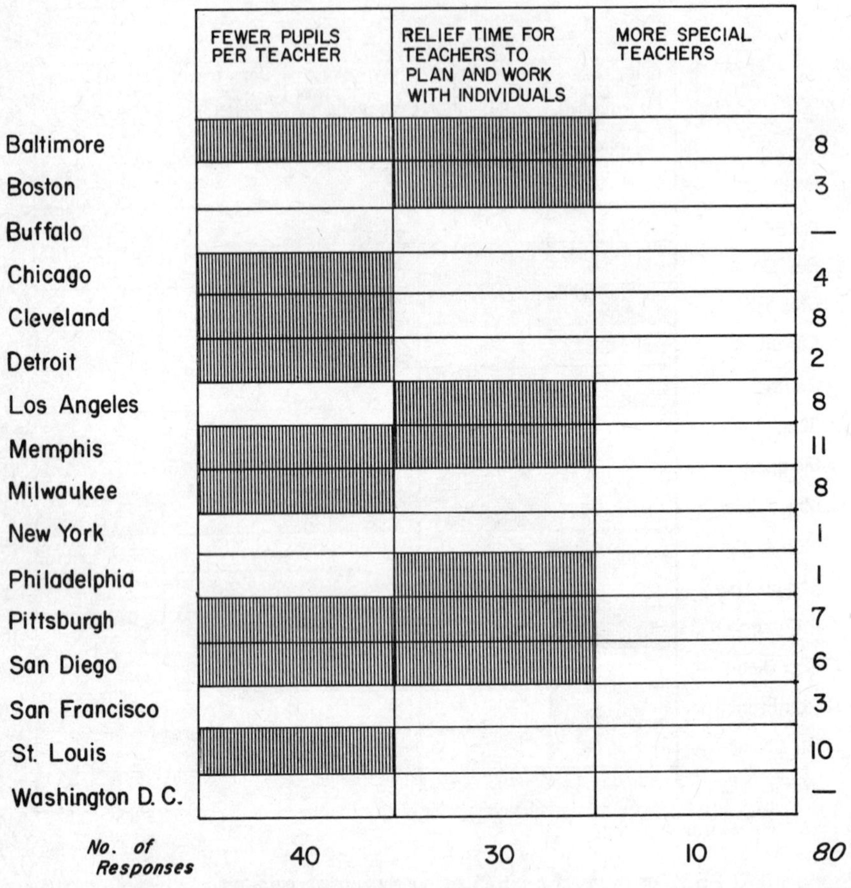

▓▓▓ 33 1/3 % or more of a city's responses concerning excessive workload of teachers

Figure 17

APPENDIX D

CITY BY CITY FINDINGS

BALTIMORE

ITV ORGANIZATION

Baltimore City Public Schools use air time and facilities contributed by commercial television stations WBAL, Channel 11 owned by Hearst, and WJZ, Channel 13 owned by Westinghouse. WMAR-TV donates limited time slots, generally used for short series or single programs aimed at the general public.

The schools produce 23 series for elementary and secondary classes and 269 adult education programs in the commercial studios. The Supervisor of the Radio-Television Department reports to the Associate Superintendent of Curriculum and Instruction.

There are seven full-time and two part-time TV teachers, who receive salary differentials as "demonstration teachers." When needed in summer months, they are paid on a per diem basis.

The Supervisor receives a differential above base salary range of $6,000-$12,600. Two Radio-TV Specialists receive lesser differentials above the same range, and are responsible for the performance of the TV teachers. A student employee on the work-study plan works three days a week as Artist. Other Department personnel are a Principal Clerk Stenographer, $4,965-$6,321; Senior Clerk Stenographer, $4,309-$5,469; and Senior Clerk Typist, $3,933-$4,965.

In 1966-67 TV operations were budgeted $150,254. $41,500 was for supervisory personnel, $71,000 for TV teachers, and $47,681 for equipment. Federal funds supplied $25,000 through ESSA and $2,452 through NDEA.

A Radio-TV Advisory Committee for the elementary division consists of principals, subject area supervisors, and an area director. Members of the Curriculum Department establish guidelines for specific subject areas. The TV teacher does research, prepares the lessons, obtains needed visual materials, writes the script and teachers' guide, reviews the script with the TV director, and nearly always gives the televised lesson without studio rehearsal.

Live lessons create some problems. When a TV teacher fainted, the Radio-TV Specialist took over, summarizing what the lesson had covered until that point.

TV teachers attend staff meetings in their subject areas, address city-wide principals' meetings, visit schools, correspond with teachers, and — rarely, because so few programs are taped — observe classroom reactions to their lessons.

The 1966 General Assembly created the independent Maryland Educational-Cultural Television Commission to develop, operate, and maintain a State ETV network. The FCC has assigned seven UHF channels. Transmitters in Baltimore, Hagerstown, and Salisbury are planned to be in operation by 1969, and those in Cumberland, Frederick, Waldorf and College Park by 1973. Capital costs, including a State production center, are estimated at $2 million. Annual operating budget is planned at about $1.5 million.

PROGRAMS AND USES

Classroom teachers' use of programs is voluntary. The Radio-TV Department does not know how extensive use of televised lessons is. From mail and requests for "give-aways" it estimates that audiences range from 6,500 to 50,000. School systems in five nearby counties use the series, as do others in Pennsylvania. Mail comes from Maryland's Eastern Shore, Delaware and Virginia.

The Mathematics Supervisor (secondary schools) had felt some classroom teachers were doing poorly, after finding instances where students were given wrong formulae and some problems which the classroom teachers themselves could not solve. In 1966-67 a series of closed circuit mathematics programs was planned for junior high schools. The programs began in the fall of 1967 after the teacher (chosen at an audition) had been given some training in TV techniques by the Supervisor and Specialists in the Radio-TV Department. This teacher is still based in the Radio-TV building. His programs are video-taped in the laboratory studios of the Community College of Baltimore with two members of the Radio-TV Department, Anna Fehl and Peter Chant, acting as directors and alternating their duties at the board. Current plans are to produce 90 new lessons a year over the next three years, geared to inner-city children. The tapes are played back in the schools at the convenience of the classroom teachers.

There is also a mathematics series for elementary school children. CONTEMPORARY MATH has been presented over WBAL-TV for several years. Jannette Dates is the teacher.

VOICEVILLE and SPEECH SCOUTS are two series on Speech Improvement. Each has 12 lessons taught by Mrs. Eileen Henderson, Speech Therapist, for grades K-3 and 4-6. The first had two additional members of its "cast", Sydney Tishler as the Postman and Mrs. Eva Jones as the Toy Shop Owner. Requests for materials offered for classroom use indicated a total audience of about 6,500. The second was taped and rented to other school systems.

BE HEALTHY! BE HAPPY! is a mental health series of 14 15-minute programs for grades 4-6 with Dr. Paul Yaffe, a psychologist, Director of Elementary Testing Services, as discussion leader.

Shirley Brown has given LET'S TELL A STORY, with 32 programs directed to lower (15) middle (10) and upper (7) elementary levels, for the past eight years.

Five Science series are YOUR WONDERFUL WORLD, taught by Mrs. Bettie Dawson for grades 1-2 and her SCIENCE EVERYWHERE for grades 3-4, each of seven lessons; SCIENCE IN ACTION, six programs taught by Peter J. Chant for grades 5-6, his seven-lesson secondary Science series on Health and Environment for junior high students, and six senior level programs for grades 10-12. A junior high NARCOTICS program was repeated on prime evening time.

LET'S SPEAK FRENCH, 32 lessons for grades 6 taught by Mrs. Ruth Menendez, was audiotaped and rebroadcast over WBJC-FM.

FOUR FACES OF DRAMA, four programs for junior and senior high schools, was presented by Sydney Tishler. One program used a Western Maryland College pantomime group. The series was rebroadcast for adult Sunday viewing.

Mr. Tishler also gave the five-program half-hour MAGIC OF LANGUAGE series for junior and senior high schools. TREASURES IN BOOKS are 11 programs for middle and upper elementary pupils, with Anna Fehl as hostess and 11 different librarians.

SYMBOLS OF OUR COUNTRY are six programs for grades 1-3 taught by Mrs. Eva Jones. HISTORY for grades 7-12 consists of programs on the Bill of Rights and contributions by Maryland Negroes, taught by Arthur L. Laupus; four programs on INVISIBLE BALTIMORE presented by Wilbur Hunter, Director of the Peale Museum (which were rerun on Sundays) and two miscellaneous programs. Mrs. Bettie Dawson gave six 15-minute lessons for grades 3-4 titled MIRROR OF MARYLAND. Mr. Laupus also teaches five lessons for upper elementary grades in the OTHER LANDS, OTHER WAYS series on Thailand, Japan and Ghana.

ACCENT ON MUSIC for grades 5-7 taught by Mr. Tishler interviewed Virgil Thomson, Aaron Copeland, pianist John Swift, assistant conductor Elyakum Shapira of the Baltimore Symphony; Spencer Hammond, Music Resource teacher, and members of the Cameo Opera Company.

One art program is in color. WHAT IS ART, six half-hour lessons for grades 5-7 taught by Mrs. Sandra Kenney, explores printmaking, ceramics, weaving without a loom, and collage for an estimated 500 classes.

For adult learning, Mrs. Naomi Bauernfeind has been teaching five half-hour programs weekly throughout the year, 261 lessons titled LEARNING TO READ for seven years. Her Friday and Saturday telecasts are for beginners, Sunday and Monday lessons for the more advanced, and Wednesdays for review. For 1966-67, to involve 2,000 adults having less schooling than grade 8, a 90% Title II B grant under the Economic Opportunity Act helped pay an estimated $53,774 expenditure, and $8,962 for July-August, 1967.

For adults LET'S MAKE A DRESS, eight half-hour lessons taught by Anne Andrews, has been taped and rerun twice as a result of requests mailed to the station.

For the general public Arthur L. Laupus is host for six Saturday afternoon half hours on HOW TO STUDY on WMAR-TV.

The single administrative use of TV is the Annual Staff Meeting for one hour in September.

Radio programs for in-school use on WBAL-FM include POETRY PARADE on 25 Mondays, with repeat broadcasts on Thursdays.

FACILITIES

The schools are guests of the commercial stations, whose equipment is excellent. There are always two cameras for every program. In 1967-68 all WJZ-TV school productions are expected to be in color; their ITV has space enough for two teaching areas or settings. WBAL-TV – the schools can use a 60' x 40' studio exclusively. WMAR-TV has excellent, full-color facilities.

The stations' art departments design and build sets, make slides, and other artwork. Their film departments assist with processing and editing.

625 TV sets are in elementary schools and 75 in secondary schools. No school has a receiver for every classroom. All 215 schools have at least one set.

In 1966-67 the schools purchased 40 RCA color TV sets, for $17,000, and Concord video tape recorders, microphones and accessories for $3,228. With NDEA funds they bought 39 RCA black-and-white TV sets for $3,795 and Concord cameras and accessories for $1,119. ESSA funds paid for $24,052 in studio TV equipment and $948 for studio lighting equipment. The color TV purchase included antennas.

BOSTON

ITV ORGANIZATION

Boston Public Schools have helped support the "21 Inch Classroom" service telecast over community ETV station WGBH, Channel 2, since 1958. They are one of 178 subscribing public, private, and parochial school systems, and now contribute $42,000 annually toward a $310,000 1967-68 budget.

The Superintendent of Schools was a member of the Educational Television Commission (since reorganized as the Massachusetts Executive Committee for Educational Television) when it was created in 1958 as part of the State Department of Education. WGBH gets no money from the State. Because of need for more air time for public television, WGBH contemplates shifting ITV to its new UHF Channel 44, WGBX, which Boston Public Schools TV sets are unequipped to receive. 1967-68 ITV schedules list only two evening programs, however, over WGBX which are repeats of WGBH telecasts.

The public schools' Director of Audio-Visual Instruction is the Board of Education's coordinator for the "21 Inch Classroom" and is responsible for the purchase of TV sets for the schools. He reports to the Associate Superintendent for Curriculum and Improvement of Instruction, who is one of the 12 members of the Massachusetts Executive Committee for Educational Television. The Committee is appointed by the State Board of Education; by law, a majority must represent member schools.

The Massachusetts Executive Committee for ETV decides what the "21 Inch Classroom" shall produce. Its Executive Director administers it. He is on the Massachusetts Committee for ITV Fixed Service to develop a master plan for 2,500 Mc. use and advise the F.C.C. on ITFS applications from the State. He is also concerned with development of a state-wide educational network.

School systems' subscriptions pay for administration, program development and production, and broadcast transmission. Membership entitles school systems to (1) brochures for every teacher, giving broadcast times and general program descriptions; (2) teacher's guides for all series a teacher uses; (3) opportunity to take part in program formulation through committees; (4) the right to tape programs off the air to be played back later, providing certain conditions are observed; (5) conferences and previews at WGBH studios; (6) teacher workshops to discuss with the TV teacher or field representative uses of new series; and (7) assistance of the field representative, who visits schools to discuss with administrators and teachers how they can use services to best advantage.

Boston Public Schools' Director of Science serves on the 20-member Programming Advisory Committee. The Director of its Art Department is on one of four Subject Area Committees set up in January, 1967 to identify the most urgent programming needs in their areas, to develop ideas for new series, and to comment on proposals submitted by other persons and groups. The Massachusetts Executive Committee for ETV has commissioned two studies at $25,000 each: one on facilities for a Statewide network, the second on management and use.

TV teachers are paid by the series, under contract, and receive a share from any national distribution. After screen-testing, WGBH and the "21 Inch Classroom" professional staff make selections from prospective TV teachers. None in 1966-67 or 1967-68 series was a Boston Public School teacher.

Pay to the non-union engineering staff is competitive with union rates. About half of the floor crew are apprentices from Boston University.

Repair of TV sets is under each school principal, usually using local servicemen.

The Director of Information obtains cooperation from commercial TV stations on news and special features. He is arranging with WGBX for a monthly half hour "SUPERINTENDENT REPORTS" series, budgeted at $1,000 per program, with plans for answering telephoned requests from the public.

PROGRAMS AND USES

In 1966-67 the "21 Inch Classroom" telecast 26 series for elementary and secondary classes and two for in-service teacher education. Its 1967-68 schedule lists 19 elementary, four junior high, and seven senior high offerings, plus ENGLISH: FACT AND FANCY for teachers. Somewhat less than 50% are locally produced, with the remainder obtained through the Eastern Educational Network.

Louise McNamara first taught ALL ABOUT YOU, the widely syndicated grade 1 Science of 11 lessons, in 1964 and nine more in 1967 with a $7,425 grant from the National Center for School and College TV. She first did LAND AND SEA, grade 3 Science, in 1963.

Anthony Saletan originally recorded SING, CHILDREN, SING for grade 2 in 1958, and revised the series in 1965 because the tapes had disintegrated. His ten of the 15 FIELD TRIP SPECIALS for grades 5-7 are in national demand.

Mme. Anne Slack's PARLONS FRANCAIS I for grade 4, and series II and III for grades 5 and 6 (sharing grade 6 lessons with Nancy Willard and Michael Jacquemin) was produced by Heath-deRochemont. The Boston Public Schools and Massachusetts Council on Education first co-sponsored this series with $100,000. Although these are probably the most widely telecast foreign language programs in the U.S., Boston schools now make scant use of them. A recent meeting, called to decide whether to continue PARLONS FRANCAIS in Boston curricular plans, was attended by four teachers.

WGBH transmits Hartford's VARIATIONS ON A LITERARY THEME and ALIVE AND ABOUT; New York's FACES IN THE NEWS, CULTURES AND CONTINENTS, and THE RADICAL AMERICANS; and Washington's THE MIME, EXPLORING OUR LANGUAGE, and ENGLISH: FACT AND FANCY.

High cost permitted production of only the first seven programs of MEET THE ARTS for grades 4-6, taught by Sonya Hamlin, with cooperation of the Museum of Fine Arts, Boston. Eight remaining programs are being done in 1967-68.

SCIENCE REPORTER taught by John Fitch is billed as a totally new version of its established series. NASA produced the first 13 programs on a $300,000 budget, about space science. WGBH produced the final 12 programs, which deal with biology, computers, and cryogenics as well as nuclear energy and telemetric communication with vehicles in space.

ACCENT ON MUSIC is an enrichment series of eight programs for junior high students. The host is Dr. Edward Gilday, Music Chairman at the State College at Lowell.

Over 250 New England teachers took part in formulation of the 12-program HUMANITIES series made in 1962. The Council for a Television Course in the Humanities for Secondary Schools, Inc. presented film copies to the "21 Inch Classroom." Clifton Fadiman leads two programs on Our Town. Maynard Mack discusses Hamlet. Bernard M.W. Knox examines Oedipus the King with scenes acted by the Stratford Ontario Players.

The Boston Public Schools' formal estimate is that 30,000 of its 55,890 elementary pupils, and 4,000 of its 37,150 junior and senior high school students, are regularly making some use of ITV. All other conjectures were that there is less use. The "21 Inch Classroom" does not keep current data on use by Boston public schools.

In 1966-67 its field representative made nine visits to schools in Boston. That year the Public Schools ordered 2,500 elementary and 1,000 secondary broadcast schedules and 1,120 teachers' guides. For 1967-68 the system has requested 2,200 schedules and 1,390 guides. The Boston Archdiocese ordered 1,700 elementary and 1,200 secondary schedules and 4,060 guides for 1967-68.

159 teachers in 16 Boston Public Schools returned survey forms in 1966-67 indicating they watched telecast series. Highest regular viewing was ascribed to EXPLORING NATURE; SING, CHILDREN, SING; PARLONS FRANCAIS; LAND AND SEA; FIELD TRIP SPECIALS, and SOUNDS TO SAY. Of 293 total Boston responses rating 18 series, there were 107 judging the listed programs Excellent, 111 Good, 54 Fair, and 21 Poor.

FACILITIES

About 148 TV sets are in Boston public elementary schools, and about 36 in its secondary schools. These are roughly one per 25 and 14 teachers respectively. Many of the sets, according to WGBH people and Boston teachers, are inoperative or of poor quality.

The Superintendent reports that Channel 44 has been offered to the Boston school system for its ITV programs. Conversion of receivers to UHF, and adaptation of direct current (which is said to be the standard electrical service in Boston's inner-city areas) to alternating current, would require — in his opinion — about $500,000 to take advantage of this offer.

WGBH had rented the second floor above a roller skating rink in an old M.I.T. building, and owned only the cameras, when a fire burned out its studios. While WGBH used Archdiocese facilities during an interim, a city-wide public campaign gained generous response. As the Superintendent puts it, "They fell into the gutter, and came out wearing a silk hat."

WGBH informants said that its new facilities cost approximately $10 million, and new buildings $2 million. There is a complete set of color Marconi cameras. Black-and-white cameras are RCA 4½" image orthicon models. Other equipment includes six videotape recorders (2 RCA, 4 Ampex), two studios, ample scene docks and shops.

The Archdiocese of Boston was the licensee of Boston's first UHF station, Channel 31, which it operated combining commercial and ETV transmissions. It has sold the license, transmitter, and one VTR to Storer Broadcasting Co. for $3.2 million, with the right to use the channel until the Archdiocese' new 2,500 Mc. system is in operation.

80% of Boston parochial schools are equipped with "RCA packages," bought on a six-year rental-purchase contract, providing every school with a master antenna and UHF converter; each classroom has a TV set. 24-hour service and insurance against fire and theft are included.

BUFFALO

ITV ORGANIZATION

The Buffalo public school system contracts with the Western New York ETV Association, which operates WNED-TV, Channel 17, on an annual basis. $36,000 per year — an average of about $.50 per student — is the basic contribution for all services.

There is an additional ESEA project, funded at nearly $100,000, to produce 90 special programs for the disadvantaged. MR. WHATNOT is one example.

WNED transmits instructional programs from 9:15 a.m. to 3:05 p.m., after which it telecasts in-service teacher education sessions until 4:00 p.m.

All subscribing school systems have their voices in making selections of programs rented from outside sources and produced by the school system on the basis of steering committe recommendations. The committee's subject area specialists and WNED staff view trial audition lessons for final selection of TV Teachers.

The teacher tapes her show with the station producer-director. About five hours are allocated for rehearsal and production of a 30-minute lesson tape. The school system releases the teacher to the station for the duration of a series. She remains on the school payroll and receives a supplementary fee of $50 per program from the ETV Association.

WNED staff consists of a Program Manager, Director of Instructional Broadcasting, and about 25 employees who receive salaries competitive with union scales. The public school system's person in charge of school television also has responsibility for coordination of federal projects.

FACILITIES AND EQUIPMENT

WNED-TV has studios on the 7th floor of a downtown Buffalo hotel. The transmitting tower on the roof is 380 ft. above average terrain. A 151 Kw. power output reaches a 40-mile radius. UHF converters on old receivers are necessary. Studio and technical facilities require improvement. More tower height and transmission power are needed. A mobile unit is desirable.

Program costs run about $1,000 per 20 minutes. Relatively few programs are locally produced.

Three men in the school audio-visual repair section perform set maintenance. The average for service is one week. There are about 265 receivers in the public schools. Every building has at least one set.

PROGRAMS AND USES

MR. WHATNOT is an Operation Horizon (Title I funds) series which won a 1967 Ohio State award. It is for pre-schoolers up through the 3rd grade.

> 90 half-hour programs seek to mitigate cultural deprivation. Puppets, live animals, music, filmed field trips, arts and crafts, objects from foreign countries, ballet, health, safety and civics programs aimed at stimulating curiosity.

This appears to be the most popular series. 90.9% of teachers and 99% of principals are reported to have expressed high enthusiasm.

EXCURSION is a locally produced series of area field trips. In 1966-67 there were televised visits to the zoo, airport and waterfront, the Weather Bureau, Niagara Falls, the Art Gallery, Science Museum, a steel plant, and Fort Niagara. A reported 9,049 pupils regularly view this offering.

FOCUS ON ART is another 1967 Ohio State award winner. Developed by Sister M. Dorothy Horan of Medaille College, the series explores the world of art, design, and architecture at grade 6 level. When art was cut from the curriculum, teachers found this program helpful in filling the gap.

Other series with reportedly extensive classroom use were COMMUNITY HELPERS (K-1), with 13,322 pupils viewing in 1966-67; Science for grades 2-3 (12,936 viewers); PHONICS I (12,616); ALL ABOUT YOU, primary Health and Science, (8,135); EXPLORING OUR LANGUAGE (7,784); PHONICS II (6,732); MUSIC IN THE AIR (6,475); SING, CHILDREN, SING for primary grades (6,280); and PLACES IN THE NEWS (5,875). These data are from the WNED-TV 1966 survey, for the entire 11 participating area school systems.

This 1965-66 material on use pointed out that participating school districts had total enrollment of 243,704 students. Programs were intended for 179,868, of whom 120,457 viewed, yielding "67% of maximum utilization."

ENGLISH: FACT AND FANCY was telecast for in-service teacher education.

Buffalo classroom teachers referred to Science, French, and Phonics telecast series as being most useful. The school administration uses television for SCHOOLS AT WORK broadcasts to the community and REPORT CARD, telecast over the Buffalo CBS station.

CHICAGO

ITV ORGANIZATION

The Chicago Public Schools pay an annual fee of $85,000 to the Chicago Area School Television Association (CAST), a regional "cross section" of school systems. CAST transmits 40 courses, rented from the Great Plains Instructional Television Library, the National Center for School and College Television, and other sources, over WTTW (channel 11) and WXXW (channel 20).

The Supervisor of technical services from the Division of Radio and Television is responsible for the supervision of all technical operations. The Consultant in charge of Closed Circuit Television from the Department of Curriculum is responsible for all aspects of instructional television in the schools. The Supervisor of technical services from the Division of Radio and Television and the Consultant in charge of Closed Circuit Television report to the Associate Superintendent who directs the Department of Curriculum Development and Teaching.

Closed Circuit TV began in April, 1962 at the Richard E. Byrd Elementary School — which had opened as an "educational laboratory" in February, 1960 — with a program financed by the Board of Education and Motorola, Inc. It telecasts courses in science, arithmetic, social studies, and language arts. In 1964 the Board of Education paid to have cables leased from the Illinois Bell Telephone Co. to link Byrd to four other elementary schools within walking distance, in the same low socio-economic neighborhood.

"Clustering" was the Superintendent's idea. Televised lessons in reading, literature, and speech were added. One advantage was that although there is high turnover of students, much of the mobility is within the neighborhood, thus mitigating some of the effects upon dislocated pupils.

In 1966, a P. L. 89-10 Title I grant provided funds to expand the Byrd Cluster by wiring 56 additional classrooms in satellite schools, by adding a non-public school to the network and by establishing 4 new clusters. Chicago's CCTV in Fall, 1967 encompassed 26 public and 16 non-public schools, with five clusters — each centering around a "studio school" — with total enrollment of 30,000 children.

There are now 15 full-time and 72 part-time TV teachers. None receives a salary increment for this work beyond pay for attending a summer institute. Each studio school has a producer-director-teacher, an ITV Coordinator, 2 technical engineers, a graphic artist, and 2 full-time television aides to operate cameras. A central office photographer provides slides as needed. Maintenance is contracted with outside firms, calling for 24-hour service.

At the Byrd Cluster, except for a full-time TV science teacher the 12 part-time TV teaching staff are classroom teachers: two in math, two in reading, one primary readiness teacher, one handwriting specialist, and three in language arts. All social studies telecasts are taped by five teachers from satellite schools in the cluster and three teachers from Byrd School.

Teachers plan programs for the coming year in the summer workshops and produce about half of the lessons on tape. The other half are telecast live. During the 8-week summer session, the television teachers at Byrd School produced 234 videotapes.

The public schools budget $188,420 for TV operation. $85,000 is for CAST, $75,000 for equipment and maintenance, $24,920 for personnel excluding TV teachers, and $3,500 for supplies. The Title I grant is $395,970: $145,000 for equipment and installation and $250,970 for operations and instructional materials.

FACILITIES

The Byrd School unit has five Motorola cameras, five years old; a Daga-Motorola console, five years old, and two modified Macktronic videotape recorders. This VTR has been discontinued. It is not compatible with most systems now in use. Spare parts are difficult to obtain. There are two receivers for each of Byrd's 36 classrooms.

Satellite schools in the Byrd Cluster have 1 television to each two classrooms. Every classroom has a cable outlet into which sets can be plugged.

Contract specifications for new clusters called for videotape recorders which are broadcast stable (suitable for eventual use with 2,500 Mc. fixed service) and color compatible. Advancements in technology have made it possible to produce a machine meeting these requirements at a price within the range of schools. Ampex has brought out a machine, the 7800, in 1-inch format, broadcast stable and color compatible.

The new South Shore High School, under construction, is equipped with CCTV as well as broadcast receivers. Each of its carrels will tune to six video and five RF channels. Other new high schools will be planned with similar systems.

There are 2,176 TV sets in elementary schools and 416 in secondary schools. All 612 Chicago school buildings have at least one receiver.

Chicago Public Schools own and operate radio station WBEZ which broadcasts on a continuous basis on all school days from 8:35 a.m. – 2:45 p.m. Programs vary in length and cover all curriculum areas.

PROGRAMS AND USES

An estimated 136,420 elementary students regularly make some use of ITV, out of 420,000 enrolled.

CAST transmits 32 series, with a total of 1,380 unrepeated telecasts. Largest reported numbers of viewers were for series intended for primary grades, but at least five courses for intermediate grades showed high use:

SERIES	GRADES	TEACHERS	PUPILS
CHILDREN'S LITERATURE	K-3	309	9,270
ALL ABOUT YOU, (Science)	1	184	7,520
ONE, TWO, THREE	K	250	7,500
ALL ABOUT US	1-3	192	5,760
GEOGRAPHY	4-6	179	5,370
ADVENTURES IN SCIENCE	5	172	5,160
STEPPING INTO RHYTHM	1-2	171	5,130
WORD MAGIC	2	170	5,100
LANGUAGE CORNER	1	167	5,010
EXPLORING NATURE	4-6	167	5,010

MODERN MATH reported 4,290 pupils in grade 1; 3,810 in grade 2; 3,900 in grade 3; 3,510 in grade 4, 3,000 in grade 5; and 2,820 in grade 6, while PATTERNS OF ARITHMETIC indicated 2,700 in grade 4; 2,520 in grade 5; and 2,340 in grade 6.

AMERICANS ALL for grades 4-8 was said to be seen by 4,530 pupils and 151 teachers, PLACES IN THE NEWS by 3,480 pupils in grades 6-8 and 116 teachers.

THE WORLD OF SCIENCE for grade 6 reported 4,350 pupils and 145 teachers; LAND AND SEA for grade 3, 3,900 pupils and 130 teachers; and DIMENSIONS OF SCIENCE for grade 7, 2,340 students and 78 teachers.

Three series of special interest, sponsored by the State Department of Education, are GEOGRAPHY FOR THE GIFTED, with 540 students in 18 classes; MATHEMATICS FOR THE GIFTED, 480 students in 16 classes; and ASTRONOMY FOR THE GIFTED, with 450 students in 15 classes.

HABLO ESPANOL had reported 720 students and 24 teachers; HABLO MAS ESPANOL 270 pupils and nine teachers. PARLONS FRANCAIS I received indications of 210 student viewers and seven teachers; its series II and III each of 60 students and two teachers.

PHYSICAL EDUCATION for grades 1-2 reported 2,340 pupils and 78 teachers. The grade 3-4 series was viewed by an indicated 690 pupils and 23 teachers.

ROUNDABOUT was telecast for pre-school and kindergarten children in the summer of 1967. In 1967-68 new programs (in Chicago) include THE WORDSMITH; YOU AND EYE, art for grades 6-8; SEARCH FOR SCIENCE, for grade 4; TELL ME A STORY for kindergarten and primary grades; and SING, CHILDREN, SING for grades 2 and 3.

The Byrd CCTV cluster produces 23 series which total 1,380 telecasts. They are said — by principals and classroom teachers — to have virtually 100% viewing by their classes. Kindergartens view 15 minutes of language arts weekly. First grades see a half hour of science and 15 minutes of language arts per week, plus 15 minutes per month for art. Second grades add a half hour of math weekly. Peak viewing is in grade 3, with 15 added minutes of social studies and a half hour on handwriting per week, plus 15 minutes of music monthly. Grade 4 omits handwriting. Grade 5 omits televised music instruction, but increases language arts telecasts to one hour per week, while Grade 6 returns to one-half hour weekly in that subject. Classroom teachers in the Byrd Cluster meet with the television teachers before telecasting begins in the fall. They receive the Instructional Television Guidebooks and information regarding pre and post telecast activities. During the school year, classroom teachers attend monthly grade level meetings. They meet with television teachers and provide feedback for the continuous program of evaluation of closed circuit telecasts.

Chicago offers four televised in-service training courses: Art without credit; Math with credit toward salary placement, both during the academic year. Summers have offered two-week workshops, increased in 1967 to 60 teachers over an eight-week period. Other uses of TV have included two in-service programs for smaller class size.

CLEVELAND

ITV ORGANIZATION

ITV operations of Cleveland Public Schools are in the process of administrative reorganization. Cleveland has had a daily schedule of telecasts for two hours over Channel 5 from February, 1962, until December, 1966. Its personnel produced and directed lessons in Art, Music, Social Studies, Health, Guidance, Science, Mathematics and Spanish.

Station WVIZ, owned and operated by the Educational Television Association of Metropolitan Cleveland, began telecasts over UHF Channel 25 in February, 1965. It first repeated programs after their transmission on commercial station WEWS. Later WVIZ took the entire responsibility for ITV.

In 1966-67 the city public school system paid $152,932 for program services of the total $280,766 WVIZ income from 39 public systems and 8 private and parochial schools. Support is based on $1 per program for grades 1-12 and $.50 per kindergarten pupil. State aid reimbursed $260,000.

Cleveland's Assistant Superintendent is one of 12 members of the Superintendents' Television Advisory Board. A Curriculum determines subject area, content, and grade levels for program series.

Three Cleveland teachers are employed full-time for television – one in Cleveland schools, two released full-time to WVIZ. They receive no salary differential for this work. Eight other teachers from Bedford, East Cleveland, Willoughby-Eastlake, and Beachwood schools, from Western Reserve University, The Plain Dealer, and Fabri-Tek, Inc. taught other televised courses in 1966.

The Mathematics Department writes its own scripts, makes a film for telecasts with three prints of each lesson available for later use by teachers in the classrooms and by groups for in-service training.

In December, 1966 the Martha Holden Jennings Foundation announced a $50,000 grant for production of secondary programs to be shown on proposed 2,500 Mc. channels.

PROGRAMS AND USES

In 1966-67 an estimated 71,588 of 111,565 pupils in grades K-8 and 1,282 of 24,514 students in grades 9-12 regularly made some use of ITV in Cleveland Public Schools. The entire regional school audience, based on the annual survey conducted by the Curriculum Council, was considered to be 331,174.

Eight series were produced by Cleveland Public Schools, 20 by WVIZ, one obtained from a regional network, and eight rented from other agencies.

Four televised courses were considered direct instruction: Math for grades 5A-6B with 8,953 viewers; 6th grade Social Studies, 7,279; 2nd grade Language Arts, 6,399, and for 6th grade, 4,052.

33 Other courses were "supplementary". Largest number of viewers were for 1st grade Music, 9,509; Safety Education for primary and elementary grades, 8,609; K-1 Story Telling, 8,436; Language Arts for grades 2-4, 7,260; Science for grades 4 (5,194) and 2 (5,133); Art for grades 1-2, 5,063; Social Studies for grades 3-4, 4,750.

Of special interest was a series for mothers of Head Start children telecast to 68 Child Development Centers; COMPUTERS AND YOU, for junior high school grades 7-9 taught by Douglas Kenney of Fabri-Tek, Inc.; Directions to all Cleveland Public School teachers for preparing the State Personnel Report; evening telecasts of Cleveland city basketball and football games, interviews with Scholars-in-Residence, and a series on THE NEGRO IN THE ARTS from Glenville High School.

For 1967-68 there will be an in-service course on THE TEACHING OF READING for grades 5-7 staff, with participation of national authorities and local specialists; four new elementary series: PRIMARY FIELD TRIPS and STORY TELLING for grades 1-2; GEOGRAPHY for grades 4-5; and SCIENCE ENRICHMENT for grades 5-6. New secondary programs will be LITERATURE and THE REAL OPPORTUNITIES for grades 7-9; HUMANITIES and LIVING IN SOCIETY for grades 11-12.

In 1967-68 there will be ten weekly 40-minute in-service training sessions for Science teachers. There will also be a 2½ hour afternoon Math program for all 6th grade teachers and principals, which can be viewed from home. Others will be in Language Arts and Social Studies.

The Cleveland Public Schools' radio station WBOE-FM transmits programs five days a week from 8:30 a.m. until 4:30 p.m. In 1966-67 these included in-service discussion of a new sequence in upper elementary Science for grades 4-6; 17 elementary, six junior high, ten senior high, and 16 supplementary series. Among elementary courses were PARLONS FRANCAIS and HOLA AMIGOS.

SENIOR HIGH GERMAN was broadcast at seven different times of day. Other senior high series were English, French, Spanish, Home Economics and Music.

Of interest to systems which use ITV for testing are Cleveland's use of FM radio for Stanford elementary and intermediate reading, arithmetic and science, Lee Clark Reading Readiness (and practice) and Digitek-Scored Tests.

FACILITIES

The ETV Association of Metropolitan Cleveland bought a new building which is expected to be in operation in the fall of 1967, and has applied to the F.C.C. for four 2,500 Mc. channels. Two Cleveland schools are equipped for closed-circuit television. One senior high school has a TV camera for local originations.

All of WVIZ's equipment is less than three years old, or new: ten image orthicon cameras, five video tape recorders, three film chains, two studios (60' x 80' and 40' x 50'), two control rooms and master control.

In February, 1967, the Superintendent estimated that the city schools had invested $115,113.20 in TV equipment, and paid about $2,500 in annual cost for maintenance and repairs. In addition, its Division of Art and Bureau of Audio-Visual Education provide services – including extensive still photography and filming – for Cleveland programs on WVIZ.

In June, 1967 there were said to be 176 TV sets in elementary schools and 86 in secondary schools, although in January it had been estimated that there were 430 receivers in 178 schools. Repair of sets is reportedly improving but is said to be still a problem.

School personnel interviewed for this study consistently stated that more sets are needed. Some said that since ITV programs have been transmitted over UHF reception is poorer.

70 elementary schools have portable listening stations: three tables with nine outlets and an audio notebook, a random access tape recorder with four tracks for recording, and four for playback.

DETROIT

ITV ORGANIZATION

The Detroit Educational Television Foundation owns and operates WTVS, Channel 56. The Public School System is one of 17 organizations which formed the Foundation in 1955, and produces most of the telecasts for which the Foundation receives $100 per school from each of 200 suburban schools. Community antenna and cable transmission firms pick up the programs and relay them to schools in other parts of Michigan.

In 1966-67 the Detroit schools provided five series of taped programs to Channel 10 in Lansing and Channel 19 in the Bay City and Saginaw area. The Archdiocese of Detroit schools has chosen seven series from Detroit to transmit from off air over their 2,500 Mc. system.

The schools' Department of Educational Broadcasting has two 2,500 Mc. channels equipped to reach 91 schools (and has two other bands reserved for future use), two translators for telecasts of Midwest Program for Airborne TV Instruction programs to 176 schools equipped to receive them, and radio station WDTR-FM. The MPATI translators must be phased out by 1969, according to an FCC regulation.

The Director of Educational Broadcasting reports to the Associate Superintendent in charge of the Division for Improvement of Instruction.

The Public Schools budgeted $428,600 for TV operations and used an additional $393,995 in federal grants. "Over $200,000" went to MPATI. Transmission rentals were between $60,000 and $70,000. $241,547 was for personnel exclusive of TV teachers, $57,838 for supplies, $22,434 for rental of programs, and $9,600 for contracted services and incidental expense.

Under P. L. 89-10 (ESEA) Title I, Detroit had obtained $255,853 for purchase and installation of TV receivers distribution systems for 178 public and 32 non-public schools, and $39,142 for a Cultural Enrichment Humanities Project.

Five full-time and five part-time TV teachers received no pay increment for this work beyond salaries, paid on a ten months' basis, ranging from $5,800 to $9,500 (with less than M.A. degree), $6,300 to $10,000 (with M.A. or equivalent), $6,600 to $10,700 (with M.A. plus 30 hours), and $6,900 to $11,000 (with doctorate).

Priorities for new programs are determined in consultation with department heads. After a TV teacher is chosen, she and the subject area supervisor make an initial course outline and work with five to seven classroom teachers developing the course and teacher's guide, in a workshop from one to five weeks. As many as 300 classroom teachers take part in orientation meetings which help introduce each new series and its revisions.

The Director is employed 12 months, at a salary that ranges from $14,235 to $17,435. Supervisors on 10 months' basis received $10,600 to $13,300; on 12 months' from $12,730 to $15,970. Department Heads got $8,700 to $11,400 for 10 months; $10,450 to $13,690 for 12 months. TV Producer-Directors on the same salary schedule as teachers, but only through the 9th step.

One Clerical Specialist was paid $6,839 to $7,420; six Stenographers from $4,939 to $6,779; two Clerk-Typists from $4,682 to $6,689. One Radio-TV Engineer received $11,305 to $12,867. Assistant Radio-TV Engineers were not listed for 1966-67 but their previous rate was $7,510 to $9,479. Technical Assistants' pay was from $6,425 to $7,156. Preparator Technicians got $5,219 to $6,218.

In January 1967 the National Program for Improvement of Televised Instruction reported on its Survey and Recommendations for ITV and Radio in Detroit Public Schools. This was directed by Professor I. Keith Tyler of Ohio State University's School of Education, who headed a survey team of ten persons.

PROGRAMS AND USES

An estimated 117,897 elementary (K-6) and 8,631 secondary (7-12) students regularly made some use of televised instruction. These were about 69.2% and 6.7% of the enrollments. 108,064 are believed to get the lessons over Channel 56 and 2,500 Mc.

The Tyler study contrasted a September 1965 survey showing 96,376 Detroit Public School students regularly viewing the schools' own telecasts and a 1966 survey indicating that over 22,000 students were regular viewers of MPATI programs with 295,000 students in various Detroit Public Schools.

Reasons attributed in our interviews for laggard use of ITV were (1) the average teacher's "print orientation"; (2) insufficient TV sets, about one for every three teachers; (3) poor TV signal, and (4) too many programs which give little that the classroom teacher cannot do without.

27 different series produced by Detroit involved 1,384 lessons. 16 of these series were repeated. First and second year Spanish had 10 and 8 telecasts weekly, OF CABBAGES AND KINGS had six, the CHILDREN'S HOUR had five, while AMERICAN HISTORY for grade 8B and ALL ABOARD FOR READING in grade 3A each had four weekly transmissions.

30 MPATI series included 16 that were repeated. One of the two Senior High social studies programs had eight telecasts weekly. 15 series had four telecasts per week.

Televised series in the first semester of 1966-67 with widest reported use were the CHILDREN'S HOUR with 11,710 student viewers and 244 kindergarten teachers; the ART LESSON for primary units (K-2), with 11,140 pupils and 315 teachers viewing, taught by Margaret Hull and produced by Peggy Van Camp; SCIENCE IS FUN, elementary science Level I, viewed by 11,052 students and 318 teachers, and REASON AND READ, with 9,739 primary students and 281 teachers viewing, taught by Ruth Harnett and produced by Miss Van Camp. All were shown at different times over Channel 56 and on Channels 10, and 12 via 2,500 Mc.

The subjects with most reported student viewers watching from three to five different course series were Science (19,991), Reading (19,082), Arithmetic (16,023), Art (11,658), Spanish (7,508), and Social Studies (6,484).

OF CABBAGES AND KINGS, the junior high humanities-oriented literature course of 36 programs funded under Title I, was viewed by 3,200 students and 75 teachers. With it was a multi-media kit over 200 films, slides, photographs, audio-tapes, records, pamphlets, articles, charts, and cut-outs, and a 100-title book kit.

Most widely viewed MPATI programs in Detroit Public Schools were LISTEN AND SAY, viewed by 3,211 pupils and 90 teachers in grades 1 and 2; SINGING, LISTENING, DOING, watched by 2,780 pupils and 80 teachers in grades 1-3; and SCIENCELAND viewed by 1,754 pupils and 50 teachers in the first two grades.

The same source tabulating the above data reported no Detroit school viewers for six MPATI series: FRANKLIN TO FROST for senior high; EN AVANT, 2nd year French; FREEDOM TO READ: OUR ADVENTURE IN FREEDOM, senior high social studies; HABLEMOS ESPANOL and PASO A PASO, 2nd and 3rd year Spanish. SPACE AGE SCIENCE for junior high had no reported viewers over MPATI, but 218 students and no teachers over 2,500 Mc.

MODERN MATH FOR PARENTS was produced at the request of the PTA Council, and shown at noon and evenings over Channel 56, which is used by the Public Schools for all daytime programming and five evening programs.

Administrative uses of TV have been the SUPERINTENDENT'S REPORT and special programs for TEACHER AIDES. Supervisors and Directors present a weekly MEMO TO TEACHERS, on new curriculum developments and methods. There have been special programs on Block-Time (6), the Growth of Business in Detroit, The Negro Artist in Detroit, Negro Literature, The Plight of the Cities, The Detroit Zoo, The Great Lakes, Children Learn Spanish, Civil War Battlefields, How to Read a Newspaper, Polling and Elections, and "God's Trombones."

About 72 individual programs for in-service teacher training included arithmetic, audio-visual aids, business education, the children's museum, curriculum laboratories, early childhood education, elementary and secondary science, English, federal programs, general orientation, legal affairs, mental health, modern math, music, press and radio-TV relations, psychological clinics, reading, social studies, Spanish, and teacher organizations. No credit is given unless the training is part of a workshop, when teachers are paid $15 a day.

FACILITIES

2,057 TV receivers in elementary schools are roughly one for every three of 6,177 elementary teachers. 721 in secondary schools would be less than one per six of 4,390 secondary teachers. A serious problem is presented by thefts. Because of the several signal sources, each outlet costs $100 in addition to the price of the receiver.

The Tyler study recommended that completely new TV production facilities be constructed, that basic TV equipment be upgraded by replacements and additions, and basic radio equipment be totally replaced. The present facility was originally a warehouse, and was vacated by Station WXYZ about eight years ago because it was obsolete and unsuited to television broadcasting.

TV equipment is antiquated. The best of seven cameras is an 11-year old GE Videcon in fair condition; the other six are from 10 to 15 years old in conditions rated between poor and very poor. Two AMPEX videotape recorders are in good condition. The 15-year-old GE audio console and 11-year-old Davis lighting dimmer board are both in very poor state. The studio has a 10-foot ceiling and pillar obstruction. Tapes stored unprotected invite fire and thefts of $150,000 invested in raw stock plus the costs of their recorded lessons.

LOS ANGELES

ITV ORGANIZATION

The Radio-TV section is under the Instructional Services Branch (other sections: Audio-Visual, Libraries, Youth Services, Safety and driver education, Science Center, and School Defense) of the Instructional Planning and Service Division. Divisional head is an Associate Superintendent, the Branch head an Administrator. Each section (which reports to the Administrator) has a Supervisor in charge or a Director.

The L.A. Public Schools budget $233,259 for ITV operations, of which $152,711 is reimbursed by the State. Exclusive of TV teachers, $118,681 is for personnel, $46,807 for equipment, $31,492 for supplies, and $115,550 for purchase of air time.

Three directors train 13 full-time and one part-time TV teachers who are classified as consultants and receive a salary differential of $66 per month during temporary assignment outside the classroom. The A-V section provides two full-time illustrators, and a photographer who prepares slides, photographs, and some films.

Radio-TV technicians help construct settings and obtain props. One secretary and two typists assist TV teachers with scripts and correspondence.

Monthly salary ranges are: Supervisor in Charge, $1,160-$1,445; TV Specialist, $944-$1,224; TV teacher, $688-$1,231; Head TV Technician, $796-$991; TV Technician, $676-$841; Senior Illustrator, $625-$775; Illustrator, $529-$658; Secretary, $405-$502; Intermediate Clerk-Steno, $345-$427; Clerk-Typist, $302-$374. Student Assistants (part-time) receive $1.49 an hour.

Some TV teachers, directors, and producers work somewhat longer than the 10-month regular pay periods, with a pay range from $1,100 to $1,000 per pay period. When they work summers, their salaries do not include the $66 increment.

In 1966-67 there was an average of 21 hours telecast per week. All except 3-½ hours weekly were transmitted over UHF Channel 28, owned by the Los Angeles Community Television Association at $250 per hour and commercial Channel 13 at $320 per hour. Commercial channels 2, 4, 7, 11, and 34 gave free time for public information and adult education. Channel 34 also telecast Spanish language lessons in English.

The school system has applied for an ESEA Title I grant of $1,290,697 to construct and activate UHF Channel 58 and $1,562,535 to produce eight new innovative series over a two-year period. To strengthen its application to the FCC for the channel, in July, 1967 the Superintendent asked the Board of Education to set aside $653,900 in local bond funds, on the grounds that the system can thereby double its use of ITV and eliminate costs for the $150,000 being spent for time on channels 28 and 13.

TV teachers, selected after auditions, must have tenure in the school system. About eight apply for each opening. Recommendations come from the principals and supervisors.

Requests for the development and broadcasting of television programs may be made by teachers, supervisors and administrators. These are reviewed by a Television Planning and Evaluation Committee. Representatives of the various operating divisions and branches; the In-Service Training Section; the Measurement and Evaluation Section; the Instructional Planning and the Instructional Services Branches serve on this committee. Recommendations for the use of TV teachers and consultants, as well as for the use of air time, are forwarded by this committee to the Television Section and to the Associate Superintendent, Division of Instructional Planning and Services.

This committee also will help to plan an evaluation of television programs.

A classroom teacher is assigned as Radio-Television Consultant for a semester. He outlines the series and writes the programs, working with a television director. After taping, the TV teacher is "encouraged" to visit classrooms for observation and making changes in the programs as required.

PROGRAMS AND USES

An estimated 297,000 elementary pupils (out of 377,233 enrolled), 1,155 secondary (grades 7-12), 1,424 junior college students attending credit courses, and 6,545 adult students regularly make some use of ITV.

A sampling of Southern California public, private and parochial school districts, released in May, 1967, found that 70,485 pupils outside the L.A. public schools viewed its ITV lessons weekly.

The largest number of televised lessons, 116, is offered in three Science series for grades 3-4, 6, and 8-9. The most successful reported series is the 60-program 6th grade Spanish required by State law. Music is offered for grades 3-5, Modern Math in 33 programs for grades 4-6. Industrial Arts is offered in series for primary and intermediate grades. Social Studies include EXPLORING LOS ANGELES for grade 3, FRONTIERS OF FREEDOM for grade 5, and GLOBAL GEOGRAPHY for grade 6.

In-service courses in Guidance and Counselling, Mathematics, and Art total 43 lessons, 16 in-service programs in Science, using four outstanding scientists, were attended by 1,200 teachers who completed written assignments for point credit.

Adult education courses include INTRODUCTION TO BUSINESS and MUSIC APPRECIATION for junior college credit, FAMILY FINANCE, CONVERSATIONAL SPANISH, and ESCUELA (English as a second language) which is said to have 40,000 viewers on Tuesdays and Thursdays and 100,000 on weekends.

Eight times a school year Radio-Television WAYS TO LEARNING appears. This is a 24-page magazine, edited by Matt Jamgochian, an ITV director who is responsible for scheduling the stations using taped series. Schedules distinguish between 24 series telecast over five channels and 16 other series presented by the County Superintendent of Schools over Channel 28 and Channel 9. The latter include French I and II; SING CHILDREN, SING; PATTERNS OF LIVING IN LATIN AMERICA; SPOTLIGHT ON AFRICA; FOCUS ON AMERICA and PLACES IN THE NEWS.

FACILITIES

The L.A. school system owns a 40' x 60' TV studio 25 feet high, and 30' x 30' radio studio, with a master control room between them. In 1964, $125,326 in NDEA funds helped make possible the purchase of equipment valued at $600,000. All is less than five years old. There are three RCA TK 60 A 4-½" image orthicon cameras, two RCA TK2 videotape recorders with remote controls, two 16mm film chains, two RCA synchronous generators with automatic changeover, two RCA 16mm projectors, a VueTronics model RK 120 Kine recorder, and an Eastman viscomatic film processor.

2,497 TV sets are in the elementary schools, 261 in junior high, 76 in high schools, 25 in college classrooms, and 30 in administration and business offices. Many were contributed by PTAs and Art Linkletter's television program. All gift sets must be accepted by the Board of Education, or the electronics section of the business division will not maintain them.

Although we heard some opinions that there is one TV set for every five elementary teachers, L.A. has 12,516 elementary teachers. The electronics section has a large workshop on San Pedro Street in Los Angeles, but tries to fix faulty sets where they are. Repair service is said usually to take one day.

Many of the receivers have rabbit ears rather than connections to building antennas, and therefore in fringe areas cannot pick up UHF signals. Specifications for construction of UHF Channel 58, for which the Superintendent has received funding authorization, call for rental of a tower on Mount Wilson.

MEMPHIS

ITV ORGANIZATION

The Memphis Community Television Foundation owns and operates WKNO-TV, Channel 10. It receives $100,000 from Memphis City Schools toward a $330,000 annual budget.

There was recently employed a Director of Instructional Television. The Memphis City Schools' Director of Elementary Education works closely with the WKNO Program Director. She reports to the Coordinator of Instruction and directs 14 Elementary Supervisors described as "generalists committed to the self-contained classroom." Her supervision appears to have gained widespread feeling that there is maximum involvement of teachers, principals, and supervisors in planning programs, work with TV teachers, in-service training, and feedback from classroom use.

WKNO makes annual questionnaire surveys of principals' and teachers' reactions. The Memphis Junior League interviews elementary teachers. Representatives of 17 West Tennessee school districts and the State Department of Education attend the annual March evaluation meeting and review WKNO proposals for the coming year.

Four regular certificated teachers are presently employed full time for television teaching. Two are Memphis City Schools' employees; two (in Art and Music) had taught in private schools. They are chosen in consultation with the WKNO Program Director, who serves as a talent scout observing teachers reported to have unusually good rapport with their pupils. TV teachers receive no pay increment for this work beyond their $5,500 to $6,800 salary for ten months' employment.

Other staff is employed on a 12 months' basis: Producer-Directors from $5,500 to $7,000; production personnel from $4,800 to $6,000; program personnel from $4,500 to $8,000; and Operating Engineers from $4,500 to $6,400.

Committees of the producer, TV teacher, and teachers from Memphis and Shelby County schools plan each new series. TV teachers prepare study guides, which are printed by July 15 and distributed to schools by early September. Production is two to six weeks ahead of the school schedule. A 20-minute lesson normally takes about two hours of studio time, costing $150 per half hour for studio crew, engineers, and tape use.

PROGRAMS AND USES

Of 67,468 Memphis elementary school pupils, an estimated 60,000 regularly received some instruction by television in 1966-67.

From 66 answers to questionnaires sent to 94 schools, WONDERING WITH SCIENCE, taught by Mrs. Osborn and Mrs. Stimbert for grades 3 through 6 showed highest comparative use by classroom teachers:

GRADE	LESSONS IN SERIES	LENGTH, MINUTES	LESSONS PER WEEK	REPEATS PER WEEK	NO. OF SECTIONS	% VIEWING
3	56	20	2	2	210	83
4	56	28	2	2	228	91
5	60	20	2	2	208	85
6	60	20	2	2	199	84

Three new series were produced in 1966-67:

THE MUSIC ROOM for grades 1 and 2 (continued from earlier years in grades 3 through 6), 60 lessons per grade taught by Mrs. Margaret Walsh. Indications of highest use (80%) were from grade 1, lowest (38%) in grade 6.

LOOK AROUND (Social Studies) from grades 3 and 4, 30 lessons of 14 minutes once a week, taught by Mrs. Joan Roth, and continued from earlier years for grades 1 and 2.

MODERN MATH for grade 6, 60 lessons, 19 minutes twice weekly, taught by Mrs. Mary Jo Harris.

CHILDREN'S LITERATURE for grade 2, a 14-minute reading by Memphis State University Speech and Drama Faculty members for 30 weeks, was used by 176 (76%) of 261 reported sections. ADVENTURES IN ART by Mrs. Roth for grades 3 through 6, each 30 lessons of 20 minutes, showed highest use (45%) in grade 5 and lowest (27%) in grade 6.

REMEDIAL READING for grade 4, 60 lessons 19 minutes long, taught by Mrs. Mary Kohlmeyer, was viewed by 97 sections.

ALL ABOARD WITH MR. B., total of 201 half-hour programs for pre-school pupils (but watched by some 1st and 2nd grades), originally paid for by the Junior League, was considered very popular with disadvantaged children.

Five high school sections viewed DRIVER EDUCATION, 29 lessons 29 minutes long, shown at seven different times on Wednesdays, rented from NET. This was the only TV instruction given 52,921 high school students.

To inform the general community about school affairs, there were 30 programs on MEMPHIS CITY SCHOOLS, including ten FACULTY MEETING OF THE AIR programs. All were repeated twice after each first telecast.

WKNO had previously used PARLONS FRANCAIS and Science for grade 7, but dropped them for lack of use.

For 1967-68 WKNO is revising Science for grade 3 and adding Social Studies and Remedial Reading for grade 5, requested by Memphis schools, as well as Math for grade 7 as a result of requests from the area ITV group.

FACILITIES

Memphis schools replying to the March, 1967 questionnaire said they had 462 television receivers, of which 38 were not in good condition. In June it was estimated that the schools had 570 receivers, and that at least one for every three teachers was available. In July, 88 new sets were reported recently delivered, and 75 others requisitioned but not yet approved because of budget cuts.

WKNO has 7,000 square feet of studio space with a 22 foot ceiling in what had been a basketball court; six TV cameras, four to 12 years old, including two 4½" image orthicons; four videotape recorders, one to eight years old, one of them a 1" RCA; two kinescope recorders; two film cameras, four and six years old; two slide projectors; two multiplexers; and a remote truck carrying three cameras.

When a Memphis teacher finds a TV set faulty, it is fixed on the spot, usually the same day. When a teachers' guide is requested, it comes on a daily truck delivery of materials arriving at every school building.

MILWAUKEE

ITV ORGANIZATION

Instructional Television in the Milwaukee Public Schools is produced and administered by the Department of Instructional Resources whose Director reports to the Assistant Superintendent, Division of Curriculum and Instruction. The Director is responsible for the overall administration and planning for television as well as audiovisual and library services.

The Production Supervisor in the Department of Instructional Resources is more directly responsible for the quality of television production and scheduling.

Four full-time and three part-time teachers are employed for television. Two with Bachelor's degrees are paid from $5,750 to $10,477 maximum. Two with M.A.'s are hired as Supervising Teachers who receive $8,300 to $11,500.

Salary schedules for the other eight television staff members are: the Director, $10,950 to $16,250; Production Supervisor, $9,450 to $13,850; Artist, $7,823 to $9,432; Photographer, $6,876 to $8,256; Photographer Assistant, $5,424 to $6,504; Senior Secretary, same; Utility man, $4,824 to $5,616, and Clerk-Stenographer, $4,152 to $5,076.

Planning a series is shared by Curriculum Supervisor, the TV teacher, and invited classroom teachers. The TV teacher takes the resulting guidelines, writes the Teachers' Guide, gives the televised lessons, and visits classrooms to observe and encourage effective use. Chosen for teaching ability and by 8-minute audition tapes which demonstrate lesson preparation, the TV teacher attends two-week summer workshops at the Vocational School studios.

All television lessons are produced and broadcast through the facilities of the local ETV station, WMVS – Channel 10. The Milwaukee Vocational Technical and Adult Schools operate WMVS (channel 10) and WMVT (channel 36). WMVS transmits about 16 hours of telecast lessons weekly to Milwaukee Public Schools and schools of the Milwaukee Catholic Archdiocese. It is NET-affiliated and cooperates on local programs with the Public Library, Public Museum, and music, art, and theatre organizations in the area. WMVT is used primarily for adult education, transmitting about three hours per evening.

The licensee is the Milwaukee Board of Vocational and Adult Education, an autonomous government unit which has taxing powers regulated by state statute. The Board consists of two employer and two employee members elected for five-year terms by the Milwaukee Board of School Directors, and the Superintendent of the Milwaukee Public Schools.

The public schools pay approximately $40,000 for station time from $123,000 budgeted for TV operations.

The Department of Community Relations within the Milwaukee Public Schools is responsible for working with commercial and non-commercial television and radio stations related to information programs about the Milwaukee Public Schools developed for the community.

EXPANDED SERVICES

In 1968 the Milwaukee Public Schools are expanding the use of media and have budgeted for the use of WMVT-Channel 36, for teaching Modern Mathematics in the junior high schools. They have also budgeted sufficient funds to initiate a feasibility study for the use of 2500 MH Instructional Television Fixed Service, and the feasibility and construction of FM radio.

PROGRAMS AND USES

The Department of Instructional Resources summarizes responses to its annual questionnaire sent to all primary and intermediate teachers in the elementary schools. It has made evaluations of the 1966 televised elementary foreign language program, of the pilot PATTERNS IN ARITHMETIC for 1960-63, and in 1960 of Milwaukee's three years' participation in the National Program For the Use of Television in the Schools.

An estimated 70,000 of 73,427 elementary (K-6) pupils make some regular use of TV, compared with about 6,000 of 49,992 students in grades 7-12.

1,330 replies to the last (February, 1966) questionnaire sent to 1,775 primary and intermediate elementary teachers said that 1,267 (95.3% of responses) used television. Highest users were 288 upper primary teachers (97%) on ARITHMETIC FOR YOU, and 207 fifth grade teachers (96%) with the mandatory Spanish course.

High use was noted by 595 intermediate teachers (87%) on ARITHMETIC FOR YOU, 701 primary teachers (86%) with ART FOR YOU, and 558 intermediate teachers (82%) using SCIENCE FOR YOU. Use of Primary Science was reported by 420 teachers (76%), Physical Education by 613 primary (75%), and 430 intermediate (63%) teachers, and Art by 444 intermediate teachers (65%).

In 1966, 78% of middle and upper primary teachers had requested Science, and 70% of upper primary teachers requested Arithmetic. Requests for 1967 were highest (78%) for intermediate Science, primary Art, (77%), and Intermediate Arithmetic (71).

ARITHMETIC

Except for experimental use in grades 1 and 2, PATTERNS IN ARITHMETIC, produced by the University of Wisconsin and taped at WHA in Madison, has been "phased out", replaced by Milwaukee-originated ARITHMETIC FOR YOU. During the 1960-63 pilot telecasts of PATTERNS to ten schools, Milwaukee organized in-service meetings throughout the first year, later televised programs for teachers every three weeks.

Conceived by Dr. Henry Van Engen, Professor of Mathematics and Education, PATTERNS first introduced modern arithmetic ideas in grade 4B with 15-minute programs on alternate days, developing lessons for grades 5 and 6 in subsequent years. Evaluation of learning achievement compared with controls found no significant difference based on established standardized tests, but differences were found when tests reflecting the new approach were used. Teachers expressed strong preference to continue the course with all or some of the telecasts. The present local programs in Arithmetic are one day each week for the third through the sixth grades.

ART

ART FOR YOU is notable. Eight lessons are broadcast to each grade level (grades one through six). The lessons are planned around Science and Social Studies being taught at each of six grade levels. All of the lessons are produced by the school system. Some children are used on the lessons. All lessons are tried out in classrooms prior to telecasts. The television teacher is one of 14 Art Supervisors whose jobs are to provide assistance to teachers.

The Departments of Art and Instructional Resources see that materials are supplied to classrooms. Of the 150 minutes allotted weekly to art instruction in elementary schools, the eight television lessons annually per grade level (15 minutes for each of grades 1-3, 20 minutes for grades 4-6) appear to catalyze learning, thinking, and appreciation of creative work. The television teacher does not find black-and-white a detriment, but looks forward to exploring the potentials of television instruction in color.

DRIVER EDUCATION

Milwaukee produces a special series of twelve television lessons in Driver Education. These lessons are used during the summer months for teaching Driver Education. Approximately 4,000 pupils are enrolled each summer for this course.

FOREIGN LANGUAGE

Trial teaching of Spanish to all fifth and sixth grades began in 1960 with television as a major teaching resource. It was evaluated in 1962 and again in 1966. First results were that pupils were able to learn foreign language patterns from television, with over 87% of 12,729 scoring higher in aural proficiency than they could have done by chance. Television lessons were shortened from 20 to 15 minutes to provide longer time for classroom follow-up, and voluntary in-service telecasts were given twice daily on designated days. The program was adopted in the Milwaukee curriculum in 1963.

FOREIGN LANGUAGE FOR YOU is now in its third cycle of revisions. Milwaukee produces its own visual cue cards and classroom recordings. Forty minutes of weekly Spanish instruction includes two 15-minute telecasts. The 1967 evaluation report is as yet available only for staff review. In general, the program compares favorably with Modern Language Association recommendations (except for fewer class periods per week) and with FLES programs in 30 other cities of 300,000 population and larger.

MUSIC

MUSIC FOR YOU offers eight lessons for each of grades 1-6. The main purpose of the series is to promote music appreciation. The series consists of locally produced programs, outstanding films, and several programs produced in cooperation with the University of Wisconsin.

HEALTH AND PHYSICAL EDUCATION

Eight PHYSICAL EDUCATION FOR YOU telecasts are given for each of grades 1-6. This program series is similar in purpose to the Art and Music series. The television teacher is one of the six Supervising Teachers in the Department of Health and Physical Education. In addition, Milwaukee uses the 11-program series on Health, ALL ABOUT YOU, produced by WGBH in Boston, for grade 1.

SCIENCE

SCIENCE TRAILS for grade 2 is designed around the concept of field trips in and around the Milwaukee area. Its purpose is to provide concrete science experiences for children at this early age. There are 12 television lessons in the series. There are 24 lessons in Science for each grade level (grades 3-6). These lessons provide the basis for the study of science in each of the units covered at each of these grade levels.

LIFE SCIENCE for grade 8 has 34 lessons. It is taught in the first semester and emphasizes the ecological approach to the biological sciences. Because of scheduling problems, all eighth grade classes cannot view the telecasts. The 1965 revision of its Teachers' Guide emphasizes films for classes not receiving television, supplementary readings from four texts including one published by the Milwaukee Public Schools, and preparatory activities with questions about biological principles and vocabulary lists of words used in the telecasts.

EARTH SCIENCE for grade 8 has 34 lessons and is taught in the second semester. The course includes geography, meteorology, and astronomy, and is similar to the Life Science series in its operation.

SOCIAL STUDIES

The only Social Studies instruction using television is PLACES IN THE NEWS, 24 lessons obtained from Great Plains Instructional Television Library, for grade 6.

IN-SERVICE

The Milwaukee Public Schools has offered a number of in-service courses produced locally and acquired from other sources. These include Personal Finance, produced in cooperation with the University of Wisconsin; Creativity, produced locally in cooperation with WMVS and University of Wisconsin – Milwaukee; Channels to Learning, produced cooperatively with the Great Plains Instructional Television Library; and, English: Fact and Fancy, produced by WETA, Washington, D.C.

ADMINISTRATIVE

Each year there is an annual Superintendent's and Board Report to the teachers. Usually the medium is used several times each year for communicating with teachers on specific issues.

COMMUNITY

Nine television programs are produced at WMVS – Channel 10, giving the Board of School Directors an opportunity to report to the community. The estimated audience is 25,000 for each program.

FACILITIES

Studios at Milwaukee Vocational Technical and Adult Schools have nine black-and-white and two color cameras; six videotape recorders (color capable), three black-and-white and two color film chains. List price of equipment owned by the VTA Schools was $1,300,400. Most of it is new.

The Public Schools have 600 television receiving sets in elementary schools and 150 in high schools. All 154 school buildings have at least one receiver. It is estimated that at the elementary level there is one set, on the average, for every three classrooms. There is hope of getting more sets through NDEA, bringing the supply to one receiver per teacher, at least in primary grades.

Maintenance of sets is considered good, with servicemen appearing within 24 hours after a complaint. If repairs cannot be made on the spot, a receiver is loaned until the classroom set is fixed.

NEW YORK

ITV ORGANIZATION

School Television in New York City centers in the Bureau of Radio and Television (WNYE-FM-TV), headed by a Director of Broadcasting. The Bureau is part of the Office of Curriculum, under a Deputy Superintendent.

WNYE-FM's 20 kw radio service, begun in 1939, continued its programs unabated in 1966-67 to supplement class instruction and provide full teaching service to handicapped.

Exploration of television started in 1949 with limited production facilities and commercial stations donating free time. From 1958 to 1962 the public schools took part in the N.Y. State Education Department's Regents ETV Project over commercial facilities leased from WPIX, Channel 11. From 1962 to 1965 city schools were the principal supporter of the school service of ETV station WNDT, supplying TV teachers and the major part of the fund required for School Television operations.

In 1965 the N.Y. Board of Education moved into its own TV production center. On April 3, 1967 its own station WNYE-TV, Channel 25, went on the air. Pending completion of Channel 25, the city continued support of Channel 13. It also used WNYC, Channel 31, the municipal station, for certain in-service teacher education courses in 1966-67.

WNYE-FM-TV has a staff of 90. 57 are specifically in TV and 29 in radio. Two Assistant Directors function in both broadcast fields: One is in charge of programming; the other supervises technical operations. There is also an Assistant Administrative Director for Business Affairs.

The TV staff comprises a Production Supervisor, 19 TV teachers, 13 engineers, 18 production people (including Directors, Graphic Artists, Film Editors, Production Assistants, Lighting Director, Announcer, Studio Technician, and Manager of Operations) and a secretarial staff of six.

For program planning, the schools' Radio and Television Council is chaired by the Deputy Superintendent for Curriculum. Among its 15 members are the Deputy Superintendent for Personnel, Assistant Superintendents for High, Intermediate and Primary Schools, Curriculum Development, and Community Education, Directors of the Bureaus of Broadcasting and Audio-Visual Instruction, the Assistant Director of Broadcast Programs, and the Supervisors of Radio and Television Production.

Reception facilities are the responsibility of the schools' Bureau of Audio-Visual Instruction, which supervises installation and servicing of television and radio sets in the schools, makes available kinescopes and audio-tapes through its Film and Tape Library Service, and is responsible for seven closed-circuit systems in the schools.

TV teachers receive $600 salary differential. They are chosen on the basis of auditions after command of subject matter and uncommon teaching ability have been verified. They are theoretically selected for one series and return to their classrooms after its completion. Sometimes a TV teacher continues in that role, visiting classrooms as an observer. She is producer, on-camera teacher, and subject area specialist who prepares lesson scripts and teachers' guides.

She does one or two lessons a week, each of which takes about a week's preparation plus two hours' studio time to set up, rehearse, and tape. Unless the taping presents problems, she does not see the lesson until it is telecast.

Eleven new programs and two to four revisions are produced weekly. Except for lessons keyed to current events, curricular TV is normally prepared about a year in advance. They try to update each series every three years, but are conscious that this often is not achieved.

The Bureau budget is $980,000. Of this, about $670,000 is for television. Unit program costs range from $100 to $2,000, with a guesstimated average of $1,000.

PROGRAMS AND USES

New York City public schools telecast 27 instructional series, with a total of 687 lessons, and 14 noon-time and after-school series for teachers in 1966-67. Of these, it produced 327 programs.

In 1965-66 the TV production center, completed in December, produced 135 videotaped programs. The annual utilization survey showed a dip, due to shifts in both TV and radio frequencies for tuning in the programs during construction of new facilities. 17,130 classes regularly watched television and 21,983 listened to radio, compared with 23,078 and 23,208 classes in 1964-65.

While normal expectation is for largest audiences in youngest grades, the 1965-66 utilization figures did not confirm this. 2,412 classes watched CHILDREN OF OTHER LANDS, taught by Mina Korn for grades 4-6. 1,272 classes saw TIME FOR SCIENCE, taught by Vera Heisen for grade 2. 1,156 classes tuned to EXPLORING SCIENCE, taught by Stephen Fisher for grade 5. 1,068 classes viewed Margaret Hodges' TELL ME A STORY, produced at WQED, Pittsburgh, for K-3, 1,062 classes used Mr. Fisher's WORKING WITH SCIENCE for grade 6.

926 classes attended ONCE A DAY WITH CHARITY BAILEY of Scarsdale Public Schools, produced by WNDT for K-3. 901 classes watched ALIVE AND ABOUT, nature study with live animals taught by Jane B. Cheney, produced by WEDH, Hartford. 700 classes followed PLACES IN THE NEWS, taught by Jerry Silverstein for grades 5-9 with prizes for the best 25 letters sent in each week, which won its second Ohio State University award. 645 classes viewed AMERICAN HISTORIC SHRINES, taught by Anne Hurrell for grades 5 and 6, produced by Mrs. Heisen and directed by Anthony Farrar, winning a Freedom Foundation award.

Large audiences regularly saw three other programs in lower grades. 627 used THE MAGIC OF WORDS, taught by John M. Robbins, Jr., produced by WETA in D.C. for grades 1-3. 600 classes viewed THE WONDER OF WORDS, taught by Elise Goodman for grades 3-4. 603 classes tuned to SOUNDS TO SAY, LETTERS TO LEARN, taught for grades 1-2 and remedial pupils by Joanne Desmond, produced by WGBH, Boston. 649 grades 1-3 heard Tony Saletan's SING, CHILDREN, SING, by WGBH.

A new 1966-67 series was OUR RIGHTS AND LIBERTIES, for grades 5-8, taught by Harry Kraus.

Some teachers of younger grades chose TV programs designed for high schools. Both YOUR PLACE IN BUSINESS and ELECTRONICS AT WORK were intended for grades 10 to 12. They had 81 and 68 classes respectively. The first of these was watched by 14 elementary and 18 junior high classes, the latter by 37 elementary and 16 junior high classes. New York has pioneered with two fall courses in vocational guidance: THE WORLD OF WORK for grades 8-10 and NEW TRENDS IN OFFICE AUTOMATION for senior high school students who have taken business subjects.

In 1966-67 WNYE telecast 14 series for teachers at noon and after-school hours, in cooperation with the Bureau of In-Service Training and subject area bureaus. It produced all but one: WETA, D.C.'s ENGLISH: FACT AND FANCY taught by James Bostain of the Department of State's Foreign Service Institute.

". . . AND GLADLY TEACH" sought to review for new teachers the many "how-to's" that are needed if theory is to be put into practice. CLASSROOM TECHNIQUES FOR INTERGROUP EDUCATION aimed at helping teachers to cope with human relations problems that arise and to promote harmonious race relations. INNOVATIONS IN EDUCATION contained five telecasts on new instructional patterns and materials.

LET'S LOOK AT FIRST GRADERS consisted of five programs; LIBRARY PRACTICES four. PROBING THE PHYSICAL WORLD dealt with chemistry and physics units of 8th grade Science; MAN, SEA AND SKY its biology and earth science units. HISTORY AND THE SOCIAL SCIENCES: BASIC CONCEPTS demonstrated teaching elements of anthropology, economics, history, geography, political science, and sociology. Other series were: GUIDING THE LEARNING OF ATYPICAL CHILDREN; MATHEMATICS, Grades 5 and 6; CHALLENGES IN FOREIGN LANGUAGE TEACHING; IMPROVING THE TEACHING OF READING; and AMERICA'S CULTURAL HERITAGE, on the contributions of different immigrant groups.

Starting in 1967-68 will be two teacher-training series in foreign languages. One will be 15 actual lessons being taught without rehearsal, with two classes: eight with bright students and seven with children who are "not language minded." The Acting Director of Foreign Languages will comment from time to time from the upper left quarter of the TV screen. A series of 30 French lessons for grade 4, supplementary in nature, attempts to obtain feedback between the TV teacher and classroom teachers.

In prospect is a series of 50 programs with narration in Spanish and English, on Spanish civilization, intended for 4th grade Social Studies and Spanish classes.

New early childhood in-service courses in fall, 1967, were planned in Social Studies and in Language Arts. One in Math is planned for spring. One new series on History and Social Studies is to be offered both over WNYE Channel 25 and WNDT Channel 13. A new Math series is for K-3, while continuing last year's course for grades 5 and 6. There will be a new Science series for grade 3, continuing those from earlier years for grades 4, 5 and 6, coordinated with 100 workshops.

The school system makes considerable use of broadcast media for community relations, organized by the Assistant Superintendent for Information Services. Every five weeks the SUPERINTENDENT OF SCHOOLS REPORTS is a one-hour program over WABC-TV, with telephoned questions from viewers. THESE ARE YOUR SCHOOLS is a half-hour program on WHN radio. SCHOOL SCOPE is broadcast daily over WABC, which gives an annual scholarship to the student who does the best job reporting school news.

Saturdays over WADO auxiliary teachers who serve as liaison with Puerto Rican students and families broadcast HINTS AND HELPS in Spanish. A TO Z is a five-minute spot announcement three times daily over WHN. EDUCATION UNLIMITED is a fortnightly half-hour over WABC.

Because the Board of Education is concerned with extending adult education, WNYE-TV anticipates added schedules from 6 p.m. to 9 p.m., offering special programs on consumer education, safety, and "Feature Stories" in cooperation with the Police Department. It does not wish to enter cultural programming as presented by the public television station, WNDT, Channel 13.

FACILITIES

WNYE-TV is a completely equipped UHF operation. Its 30 kw transmitter has a GE helical antenna sharing a 690-foot tower. With power gain of 25, and expected effective radiated power of 750 kw, fall 1967 tests measured ERP of better than 670 kw.

At the studio are three RCA TK60 image orthicon cameras, three RCA videotape recorders, two Ampex VTRs for playback at the transmitter, a film chain, and a 45' x 60' studio fully equipped with rigging and lighting gear, rear screen projection, dressing and makeup rooms, technical and scenic workshops. There are separate graphic arts sections and film screening and editing quarters.

Contrasting with excellent production and transmitting equipment is generally poor reception. This was said to arise primarily from inadequate antenna installations. January, 1967 inventory of 672 out of 861 schools found 3,574 TV sets (most schools having 2, 3 or 4 receivers), 2,104 of which were less than five years old. 50 schools had no UHF sets. The average rated quality reception was less than fair. Even among new sets furnished with ESEA funds, only five out of 30 school districts reported good reception. 226 schools reported poorer reception of Channel 25 than with UHF Channel 31. Until schools are installed with UHF antennae and outlets, this situation will persist.

Best conditions may be in Brooklyn, where three school districts reported excellent reception in four elementary schools and good reception in 24 of 42 elementary schools, three of five junior high schools, and three of four high schools.

Maintenance of ITV receivers is from funds available to the principal for minor repairs, and is generally done by commercial servicemen.

PHILADELPHIA

ITV ORGANIZATION

The three former Divisions of Libraries, Audio-Visual and Radio-TV have been consolidated into the Division of Instructional Materials. The Director reports to the Associate Superintendent of Instructional Services.

The Board of Education contracts with WHYY, Inc., the non-profit corporation which operates Channels 12 and 35, for studio production and transmission services. The appropriation for 1967-68 is $563,000 for the hours 9 a.m. to 4 p.m. and thirty minutes in prime evening time five days per week.

Monies for TV teachers, artists, photographers, and materials come from the Board of Education budget, and total about $275,000 per year.

Feedback sheets accompany monthly published schedules. The Director analyzes returns, which are also checked by staff members whose lessons are discussed in these responses. Priorities for programming are established by polling teachers, principals, and curriculum specialists each year, in or near February. From these polls, the Associate Superintendent, Director of Instructional Materials, and curriculum staff make final evaluations of needs.

Seven full-time TV teachers are former classroom teachers classified as Radio-TV Assistants. They are employed on a 12 months' basis, at the level of supervisors on the salary schedule. Five temporary TV teachers are on loan to the Department, receiving their teaching salaries plus $400 per year. One summer teacher for two Literature series for grades 1-4 and 5-8 received $1,800 for 24 programs. Three teachers serve part-time.

The TV teacher plans, writes (with a curriculum committee), and produces the series, plans visuals for preparation by two artists, and appears on camera. A director spends from one to two hours in final preparations. When a program is considered ready for telecast, it may be presented live, or on tape (reportedly about 50% each).

PROGRAMS AND USES

An estimated 200,000 Philadelphia Public School pupils regularly view one or more instructional programs per week of the 1,012 hours offered annually for instruction, teacher training, adult education, and public relations.

Programs offered for elementary pupils include Social Studies, Science, Language Arts, Art, Music, Geography, stories, Speech Improvement, Spanish, and French.

Junior High School programs include Mathematics, Science, Government, Developmental Reading, Literature and Careers.

Senior High School programs include Biology, Economics, Literature, History and Fine Arts.

The use of TV for in-service education is increasing. Mathematics, Reading, French and Intergroup Relations have attracted 12,000 teachers.

Adult education programs include **Operation Alphabet**, planned to combat illiteracy; and the **High School of the Air**, to give credit toward a high school diploma, or to permit an out-of-school adult to take an examination for an equivalent diploma. A series for parents of pre-school children, particularly in poverty areas, was presented "to improve the learning climate in the home."

Weekly public information telecasts inform citizens about school problems and activities. When appropriate, the three telephones are used in the studio, where citizens may call in questions during the telecast.

FACILITIES

An ESEA grant has added 2,000 TV sets, bringing those in Philadelphia Public Schools up to about 3,500. By January 1, 1968, 180 school buildings will be wired to receive TV signals, with one set per three rooms and an outlet in every room. 70 more will be wired when funds become available.

Because of bulk purchases and school specifications (no antennae in sets, but equipped to take signal from wall outlets), new receivers cost $99 each. The lack of antenna reduces likelihood of theft.

WHYY has three RCA TK60 4½" image orthicon cameras, two Norelco color plumicon cameras, six Marconi 4½" image orthicon cameras (donated by CBS), three GE 3½" image orthicon cameras, three Ampex videotape recorders in Philadelphia, and three Ampex VTRs and a remote band in Wilmington.

Channel 12 was assigned to Delaware. Its transmitter is in Glassboro, New Jersey, but will be transferred to Roxborough, Philadelphia, where the commercial transmitters are located.

The Tri-State Broadcasting Council is comprised of schools in New Jersey and Pennsylvania. Participating schools pay $1.00 per pupil, for which they receive teacher guides. The Council pays for recorded programs from other centers.

Philadelphia Public Schools permit these recordings on its block of time on WHYY. Curriculum committees from Philadelphia and Tri-State schools plan and produce programs cooperatively.

Commercial station WFIL-TV donates time and facilities for five TV courses weekly (plus a sixth on alternate weeks), and radio stations WFIL and WFLN make possible ten in-school programs weekly. The "WIFFIL Schoolhouse" began on radio in 1943 and on TV in 1948; it has won five Freedom Foundation awards. The station prints and distributes 10,000 manuals written by the schools' Radio-TV staff. There are about 3,000 classroom radio sets.

From October 17 to November 18, 1966, WFIL telecast its series in color. Five manufacturers — Admiral, GE, Philco, RCA and Zenith — lent 40 receivers which were distributed among all school districts. The color was considered good. Pupils and teachers reported that color makes a real difference in Science and Art.

The State of Pennsylvania has allocated about $1 million annually for ETV since 1964. There are now seven stations, compared with two in 1962.

A feasibility study for a 2,500 Mc. facility by Jansky and Bailey has been completed. Eight channels would be used to provide four channels to each Philadelphia school. Four would transmit to the south and four to the north, to avoid interference by tall center city buildings. The study takes into consideration channel assignments for Temple University, University of Pennsylvania, the Community College, Diocesan Schools and four adjacent counties. The channels would be used for repeats of programs for more flexible viewing, for distribution of special programs to special segments of the audience (among them, Puerto Ricans), and to distribute film and tape material to carrels for computer-assisted instruction.

Conwell School is one of eight "magnet" schools in Philadelphia being enriched in personnel, materials, and innovative ideas. Now serving grades 2-8, in two years it will be wholly for intermediate grades 5-8 with 600 pupils, 200 bussed from other parts of the city. Renovation of the old building has removed walls to make larger rooms for 125 to 150 pupils each.

Like all 34 TV Coordinators in closed-circuit schools, Conwell's is an enthusiastic housewife receiving a salary of less than $100 weekly. A studio, half classroom size, is linked by cable to all classrooms. A GE camera and Ampex VTR are wired to 29 TV sets in the building. The entire CCTV facility cost about $15,000 per school. 60 half-hour tapes cost $1,800. It is used to record live programs or films for later replay or for in-school production. Cameras are used to permit pupils to view themselves after a talk has been recorded. This technique is used for speech improvement, oral expression, and for writing for TV presentations.

The cameras can also be used for Micro-teaching, through which a teacher may evaluate herself with a series of recordings of her (or his) teaching procedures and techniques.

PITTSBURGH

ITV ORGANIZATION

In-school TV lessons began when the community ETV station WQED opened in April, 1954. Owned by Metropolitan Pittsburgh Educational Television, it involves school districts and parochial schools of ten western Pennsylvania counties, 6 West Virginia counties, and 1 Ohio county, operates WQED, Channel 13, and WQEX, Channel 16. Pittsburgh Public Schools pay $70,000 toward WQED School Services' budget of $222,164.

In the Public School system, the Associate Director of Learning Resources for Television and Radio Education reports to the Associate Superintendent for School Services. The Associate Director, the

Director of Instructional Services, and the Associate Director of Instruction for General Elementary Education serve on the School Curriculum Advisory Committee. This committee meets at least once a month, calls upon consultants as needed, and decides on courses, TV teachers and schedules.

There are also active Curriculum Development committees for each Pittsburgh-originated course. 4th grade Science has a Pittsburgh elementary school principal on its committee of six, for example; 5th grade Science had two Pittsburgh principals. The Secondary Developmental Reading Committee had the Pittsburgh Supervisor of English and professors of education from two area colleges as its committee of five.

Four full-time TV teachers in 1966-67 received regular teachers' salaries, at scheduled rates from $5,600 to $11,000 plus a 10% differential for this work. Other salary ranges are: Associate Director, $10,320-$13,200; TV Supervisor, $8,300-$10,700; and Television Repairman $5,448-$6,960.

WQED has on its School Services staff a Director, an Assistant Director for Utilization and Development, an Assistant Director for Programming and Operations, a Producer-Director, and three secretaries. Under its Executive Director of Broadcast Operations are an Art Director, three Artists, one construction man, and a photographer.

The 1966-67 school budget had $117,524 for financing TV operations, not including TV teachers. $28,124 was for personnel, $17,000 for equipment, and $2,400 for supplies. In addition there were two ESEA grants: $49,950 under Title I, and $5,000 under Title III.

PROGRAMS AND USES

Pittsburgh estimates that 28,000 of its 50,484 kindergarten through 6th grade pupils, and 10,000 of its 31,226 junior and senior high students, are regularly making some use of ITV. These data are derived from questionnaire responses which showed 111,488 "student participations," a cumulative figure with some students (especially in primary grades) viewing two or more series. This is about one-sixth higher than in 1965-66.

There were 3,118 "class participations," also a cumulative total. 919 of Pittsburgh's 2,713 teachers reported using one or more ITV series.

The Curriculum Advisory Committee has all ITV courses identified as being (a) basic instruction, (b) enrichment instruction, or (c) in-service education.

To achieve the purpose of basic instruction the WQED teacher's guide states that students should view every TV lesson. For enrichment, use

> "may be either sequential or selective, depending upon the primary purpose of the course design. For example, TALKING TOWN is a sequentially-developed enrichment course with an increasing complexity in the language development patterns presented throughout the year. CHILDREN OF OTHER LANDS, however, is designed for selective utilization. Each lesson is a complete unit and classroom teachers should use the television lesson only when it can be used as an integral extension of the learning experience.
>
> "Other enrichment courses are most complex in design. PEOPLE AND THEIR WORLD is developed so that classroom teachers can be selective in the choice of units to be utilized. However, once a unit has been chosen, each lesson within the unit should be used sequentially."

QED KINDERGARTEN is presented for pre-school children who do not have the opportunity to attend kindergarten.

Pittsburgh schedules some ITV lessons so that teachers can preview them prior to group viewing in school. NEWS 67 was shown Thursdays at 1:40 p.m., Fridays at 9:15 a.m. and 10:30 a.m. for classes, with teachers' previews Wednesday at 5:50 p.m. and Thursday at 8:10 a.m. In-service courses are telecast during noon hour, early morning, early evening and Saturday mornings. Each lesson is repeated at least once, to allow for choice of home or school viewing.

There were three in-service courses in 1966-67. FORM AND IMAGINATION is 33 half-hour lessons on the creative approach to primary and intermediate art, taught by Mary E. Sceiford of Mt. Lebanon Public School. PATHWAYS TO DISCOVERING MUSIC (taught by Prof. Charles Leonhard of the University of Illinois, produced by the Georgia ETV Network, and rented through the National Center for School and College Television in Bloomington) presents four sessions on a pattern for teaching music to elementary grades. ELECTRONICS AT WORK is 90 lessons, taught by John W. Wentworth for "teachers of industrial arts and/or high school students at the 11th or 12th grade levels."

No ITV in-service training courses are required or assigned. No college or salary credits are offered.

Of 24 ITV series comprising 842 lessons in 1966-67, 9 series and 332 lessons are grouped under English & Language Arts, five series and 241 lessons in Science, five series and 107 lessons in Social Studies. Pittsburgh does not use ITV for Math, History, or Foreign Languages.

BEGINNING RESPONSIBILITY is seven lessons for primary grades on being on time, obeying rules, being quiet while engaged in routine activities, respect for others' property, taking care of things used in the classroom and playground, and proper care and handling of books.

TELL ME A STORY, taught by Mrs. Margaret Hodges, formerly of the Carnegie Library's Boys and Girls Division, is used by school systems around the country by rentals through the National Center for School and College Television. Mrs. Hodges is a story specialist in Pittsburgh Public Schools' Compensatory Education Department and lectures in **Storytelling** at the University of Pittsburgh School of Library and Information Services.

TALKING TOWN is a course of 36 lessons in speech for kindergarten and 1st graders, with some content adaptable for grades 2 and 3. Vaughn Weber and Jane S. Crockett alternate sequences of nine lessons.

All five Science series are considered basic instruction. SCIENCELAND for grade 2, taught by Barbara Yanowski, is rented from MPATI. Francis A. Alder of Keystone Oaks Schools teaches three series. He gives 61 20-minute lessons for grade 4 with sequences on plants, animals, the earth's place in the solar system, air and weather, simple machines and energy. For grades 5 and 6 he has different series, each 49 25-minute lessons, varying in their allocations to Earth Sciences, Space Science, Physical Science, Life Science, and Applied and Related Science. EARTH AND SPACE SCIENCE (taught by John D. Wells, produced by the Junior High School Television Council of St. Paul, and rented through the Great Plains ITV Library in Lincoln, Nebraska) is 50 lessons on Astronomy, Geology and Meteorology.

The Illinois Television Project for the Gifted geography sequence for advanced 5th and 6th graders, rented through the Great Plains ITV Library, is offered in Pittsburgh to students who are two years ahead of grade level in reading ability, have scored 125 IQ, have high grades, and are recommended by their teachers.

Pittsburgh uses MPATI's LEARNING OUR LANGUAGE for grades 3 and 4 taught by Assistant Superintendent Adah Miner of Shoreline Public Schools in Seattle. FRANKLIN TO FROST, American Literature for senior high students taught by Dr. Arthur Eastman of the University of Michigan. It rents THE HUMANITIES through Encyclopaedia Britannica Films; WGBH Boston's SING, CHILDREN, SING and ALL ABOUT YOU for the primary grades; WNYE New York's TIME NOW FOR MUSIC for grades 3 and 4 and CHILDREN OF OTHER LANDS for intermediate grades; KRMA Denver's AMERICANS ALL for upper elementary grades; and WETA Washington's EXPLORING OUR LANGUAGE for grades 5 and 6.

PEOPLE AND THEIR WORLD, seven Social Studies units taught by Robert E. Honse of Chartiers Valley Joint Schools for grades 6 and 7, is identified as suitable for "selective utilization" of particular units but requiring "sequential utilization" of lessons within the units. There are two teacher previews the week before each Monday; a 20-minute lesson, with repeat programs three times a week.

On UHF Channel 16 are LANGUAGE: SENSE AND STRUCTURE, an introduction to the "new" grammar for grade 9 and LANGUAGE: PATTERNS IN MOTION for grade 10. Taught by Robert Berkebile, each has one lesson per week repeated seven times on the same day of the week.

DEMAND PERFORMANCE is a series of 64 films shown twice weekly for primary grades and twice weekly for "all others" — elementary, junior and senior high schools.

FACILITIES

In 1966-67 WQED had two studios (65' x 35' and 30' x 23') with separate control rooms; six RCA cameras, one or two years old; five RCA videotape recorders, two to seven years old; and one RCA and one GE audio unit, both about seven years old.

New studios are expected to be ready for use in 1968.

There are three Marconi color cameras. Two mobile units exist: one about the size of a bread truck, carrying two cameras and a VTR; a larger truck with four black-and-white cameras or three color cameras and two VTRs.

In June, 1967 there were 718 TV sets for 1,463 elementary (grades K-8) teachers, and 152 for 1,250 secondary (grades 7-12) teachers. The primary and intermediate teachers interviewed stated that there were not enough sets, and those available were often out of repair and gave poor reception. A booklet on use of TV for teachers lists one telephone number to call when a set needs repair, and a second extension to call if service is not had within 48 hours. In November, 1966 there were three master antennas in elementary schools, eight limited antenna systems (for three to eight rooms) in secondary schools, and money encumbered to install limited antenna systems in eight elementary schools. Pittsburgh has 111 school buildings.

A January, 1967 study by a consulting firm investigated comparative costs for ITV distribution systems using videotape, 2,500 Mc. Fixed Service, and leased cable. It concluded that the optimum system would be 2,500 Mc. service with a relay located at Station WIIC, a studio-to-transmitter link leased from Bell Telephone Co. of Pa., and an intra-school distribution system purchased from a qualified electronics firm. The 10-year cost estimate was $1,526,292. Alternatives were computed at $3,531,566 and $8,312,102. Instructional factors did not appear to be considered.

ST. LOUIS

ITV ORGANIZATION

The St. Louis Educational Television Commission owns and operates KETC, Channel 9. The Board of Trustees has 11 members, two of whom are non-voting members selected by the Advisory Council, which is appointed by the Chairman. The Mayor and County Supervisor appointed the first Board in 1954. It has since been self-perpetuating.

Six members represent the community-at-large. The Superintendent of Schools of St. Louis Public Schools, one superintendent selected by the Superintendents of Cooperating School Districts of St. Louis County, and a representative chosen by the Higher Education Coordinating Council are *ex officio* members.

St. Louis Public Schools contributed $100,000 toward the Commission's annual budget of $350,000 in 1966-67 and $400,000 in 1967-68.

KETC serves 26 school districts. During past financial difficulties, the station sold its cameras to meet payroll. It now produces no programs. Groups of about 15 teachers, supervisors and principals preview available series. Further selection and scheduling are decided by the advisory committee on school programming, and six curriculum people from public, parochial and county schools.

PROGRAMS AND USES

St. Louis school people said the following series were useful:

ROUNDABOUT and ONE, TWO, THREE at the primary level. The latter features a puppet for once weekly 15-minute reading readiness enrichment telecasts.

SCIENCELAND (Grade 1) and SCIENCE CORNER (Grades 2-3) encourage curiosity with focus upon every-day subjects and phenomena.

DRIVER EDUCATION (7-12), a seven-week series four times per week through half-hour films, is well received.

The Superintendent's annual report, HARD TIMES AND GREAT EXPECTATIONS, was telecast on two separate showings. Both in its taped form, and as a printed brochure, this could be a model for other Great Cities. Dr. Kottmeyer sets forth worsening urban school problems with force and eloquence, but with enough specific reasons for hope, and witty allusions to earn respect.

Few school people we interviewed felt there was consistent or frequent use of TV in classrooms.

KETC reports that in 1966-67 St. Louis City schools ordered 9,811 teachers' guides out of 20,003 guides ordered by schools in the region, for 34 series: ten series for primary grades, nine intermediate, 12 junior high, and three for high schools.

Its survey for 1965-66 used a questionnaire. 1,611 teachers in 134 of 154 surveyed schools reported uses. Extrapolation at 35 pupils per class estimated 210,245 total student usage. The analysis separated regular from occasional use, and grouped teachers' written comments on program quality.

Data from the two report:

SERIES	1966-67 ST. LOUIS CITY	(1966-67 REGION)	1965-66 REGULAR USERS	1965-66 OCCASIONAL	EXCELLENT TO GOOD	MEDIOCRE TO POOR
PRIMARY						
The Friendly Giant	542	(1,021)				
Seeing, Listening, Doing	538	(1,039)	501	172	45	16
The Road to Reading	521	(1,123)	551	131	107	8
Scienceland	516	(1,131)	614	194	114	11
Stories	460	(862)				
Science Corner	402	(958)				
Land and Sea	337	(801)				
Initial Teaching Alphabet	317	(508)	87	59	8	3
Why and How	278	(637)	280	146	50	3
One-Two-Three	243	(508)	520	89	79	2
INTERMEDIATE						
Americans All	384	(880)				
Our Land	361	(851)				
Exploring With Science	358	(882)	702	118	109	2

SERIES	1966-67 ST. LOUIS CITY	(1966-67 REGION)	1965-66 REGULAR USERS	1965-66 OCCASIONAL	EXCELLENT TO GOOD	MEDIOCRE TO POOR
Quest for the Best	355	(921)				
Learning Our Language	350	(750)	246	68	34	-
Music for You	348	(658)	172	107	15	4
Learn to Spell	334	(706)	130	52	22	6
Intermediate Geography	273	(666)				
I Like to Listen	263	(599)	136	78	21	6
JUNIOR HIGH						
Places in the News	329	(631)				
Science Reporter	310	(581)				
Adventure of Science	250	(503)				
Advanced Mathematics	233	(387)				
American History Films	231	(315)	140	93	35	-
This is Missouri	211	(331)	70	37	12	-
Jr. High Geography	205	(374)	85	66	20	-
Advanced Astronomy	192	(288)				
Art	169	(222)	56	27	11	2
Advanced Geography	154	(288)				
Pathfinders	154	(226)				
Missouri Constitution	148	(224)	100	31	11	-
SENIOR HIGH						
Franklin to Frost	30	(52)	97	26	32	-
Newspaper Staff Meeting	12	(30)				
Driver Education	3	(10)	20	6	-	-
TOTALS	9,811	(20,003)	4,507	1,500	725	63

FACILITIES

KETC-TV Channel 9 was one of the first ETV stations to go on the air. Its transmitter is an old water-cooled installation which used to have considerable down-time when it was not functioning, but since reorganization this has not been more than 15 minutes per school year.

The station has raised matching funds for a new transmitter. These are now in the bank, earning interest. It has bought land for a new transmitter, and submitted application to the U.S. Department of Health, Education & Welfare for funds under the ETV Facilities Act. The non-profit corporation hopes that during the 1967-68 school year signal power will increase from 144 to 316 kw.

The station provides the services of an engineering consultant and technical assistance to schools during the summer for improvement of antenna systems.

SAN DIEGO

ITV ORGANIZATION

Between 1952 and 1956 San Diego City Schools conducted an experimental ITV project, producing nearly 300 telecast lessons – touching all curriculum areas at grade levels K through 12 – in cooperation with commercial stations KFMB, Channel 8, and KFSD (now KOGO), Channel 10. Although the FCC had tentatively assigned VHF channels 3 and 12 for a proposed ETV facility, these were lost by default.

In May, 1966, the San Diego Unified School District received an ESEA Title III grant of $181,171 to develop 128 videotaped ITV programs and to acquire syndicated programs for all San Diego County school districts and non-profit private schools. In October, 25 districts joined in forming the San Diego ITV Authority, which went on the air – temporarily using commercial station KAAR, Channel 39 – on January 31, 1967.

Members' fees, based on 75c per average daily attendance, should be $187,000 for 1967-68. Of this, 25c per pupil is returnable by the State Department of Education under the Farr Quinby Act. Toward the ITVA budget, San Diego City Schools budgets $100,000.

Receipt of project funds stimulated San Diego State College to construct its 1 million watt facility using Channel 15. A contract with the College obtains studio facilities at $143 per hour, broadcast time at $105 per hour, recording and playback at $37 per hour, technical and production personnel.

For 160 broadcast days from September 25, 1967 through June 3, 1968, $40,755 is allotted for studio use, $67,200 for time, $29,600 for recording and playback, $6,000 for videotape stock purchase, and $27,800 for teacher consultants.

A Representative Council, consisting of one member for each of 26 member school systems – out of 47 in the county – plus one added member for each 10,000 average daily attendance, sets policy.

The Council elects a seven-member Executive Committee which meets monthly to transact business concerning fiscal, personnel, and other matters. The General Manager serves as secretary to this executive board of the Authority, reporting to and receiving direction from it.

A Joint Curriculum Coordinating Committee, with one professional educator appointed by each member school district, advises on all matters pertaining to program and materials developed by the ITVA. Course selection is decided by the ITVA Executive Committee: three from San Diego Unified School District, three from other districts, and one chosen by the County Dept. of Education. It appoints a Steering Committee of 13, which guides the work of the JCCC and makes recommendations for programs to the Executive Committee.

Study Committees, now 13 in number, make program recommendations in Art, Foreign Language, Language Arts, Mathematics, Music, Science, Practical Arts, Vocational Guidance, Health Education, Physical Education, Social Science, Pre-School and Special Education. They view available series from other sources, suggest programs for local production, and recommend which subject areas do not require ITV.

ITV operations are in the province of the Assistant Superintendent for Curriculum Services. The ITV Authority has a General Manager whose salary range is $15,000-$17,000. There are a Project Evaluator at the same pay, an Educator-Producer ($12,000-$14,000), and four full-time TV Teachers ($6,500 to $10,000) without salary differential, an Editorial Coordinator ($8,500-$10,500), three Secretaries (at $5,250-$6,500 and $5,000-$6,250), a Photographer ($8,500-$10,000), two Artist-Illustrators ($5,000-$6,500), secretarial and clerical help used at peak periods at $2.25 and $1.85 per hour.

In-service courses are offered for college credit, although because of a limited number of receivers and reception problems they are neither required nor assigned.

PROGRAMS AND USES

An estimated 50,710 elementary (K-6) out of 72,028 enrolled and 33,431 secondary (7-12) out of 49,100 enrolled students regularly make some use of ITV.

An evaluation team developed a questionnaire, reviewed by curriculum area study committees, interviews of teachers and administrators, and collected anecdotal material by mail and telephone. 1,400 elementary and intermediate/secondary teachers received questionnaires (distributed to one out of every ten teachers) requesting opinions on the merit of study guides and programs on 14 in-service series and 28 series directed to students from January 30 through May 29, 1967. There was a 21% return: from 205 elementary and 94 intermediate/secondary teachers, or 2.1% of the student-teacher population in 26 county and city school districts.

The highest rated series were ALL ABOUT YOU, the series of 11 Biology lessons for grades 1-2 produced by WGBH, Boston, distributed by the National Center for School and College Television; AMERICANS ALL, 31 20-minute programs on American History for grades 4-6 from KRMA, Denver, through the Great Plains ITV Library; PHYSICAL EDUCATION AND TESTING, eight locally-produced programs for grade 5; YOU AND EYE, the first 16 programs in Art for grades 4-6 from KQED, San Francisco, through the NCSCTV; 60 lessons from OF COURSE WE SPEAK SPANISH for grade 6 from Los Angeles City Schools; PROCESS TO PRODUCT, six locally-produced lessons on Science Creativity for grades 5-6, and 34 lessons in GEOGRAPHY for grade 4 from KRMA, Denver, through the Great Plains Library. They received from 7.2 to 7.78 on a 0-10 scale, in the opinion of teachers.

PROCESS TO PRODUCT was an experimental trial of eight 20-minute programs exploring the methods and materials devised by J. Richard Suchman of the University of Illinois and Science Research Associates to develop inquiry in physical science. There were a workshop to brief teachers in the inquiry method and ITV techniques, selection of eight children from each class as student participants, practice sessions by teachers and classes, a pilot program with Dr. Suchman as TV teacher, use of stimulating "discrepant events" and — by some teachers — six SRA problem films, programs presented by seven different teachers for 16-17 minutes with viewing classes asked to continue the dialogue and (on the last three lessons) participation by viewing students from five different school locations via a 360 degree telephonic audio loop.

Scores on a creative thinking test devised by Willis Robinson, U.S. International University psychologist, and the Creative Writing Test administered to two experimental groups — six classes which took part and viewed, six which only viewed — and five grades serving as a non-viewing controlled group produced "a sizeable and significant increment in creative behavior." Increases measured by the Robinson test results, analyzed by constant group and random split half-methods, were reported above the .01 level of statistical significance. The ITVA will produce 36 PROCESS TO PRODUCT programs in 1967-68, retitled CROSSROADS.

Five other series locally produced in the spring, 1967 were PEACEFUL USES OF ATOMIC ENERGY, 13 "general enrichment" programs for grades 5-12; NEWS OF THE WEEK for grades 4-6 and NEWS REPORT for grades 7-12, each of 15 programs; A HEALTHY YOU, 6 health and physical education programs for grades 1-2, and TODAY WE PRESENT twice weekly general enrichment programs for grades K-14. Some of this last series' programs were obtained from outside sources.

Entire series rented from outside sources in 1966-67 included PLACES IN THE NEWS, weekly 20-minute programs from WNYE, N.Y. through the Great Plains Library; eight FOLKLORE and 30 THROUGH CHILDREN'S EYES, enrichment programs for grades 4-8, and 15 IMAGES OF AMERICA and 16 MAKING OF MUSIC programs for grades 9-12, from the University of Michigan; 30 CHILDREN'S LITERATURE programs for grades K-3 from KUON, Nebraska through the Great Plains; ALL THAT I AM, 32 programs on creativity for grades K-3 from MPATI; and 12 LOOKING AT LANGUAGE programs in Language Arts from Minneapolis Public Schools for grades 7-9.

In-service series in 1966-67 were ENGLISH: FACT AND FANCY, 15 lessons from WETA, Washington, D.C. through the NCSCTV and CHANNELS TO LEARNING, 10 programs on use of ITV produced at ten Midwest Centers under the stimulation of the Great Plains Library.

Other in-service programs were 12 telecasts of CANFIELD SPEAKS (on Language Arts) and eight PHYSICAL EDUCATION AND TESTING for teachers of grades 4-6; five each on TO TOUCH A CHILD and INTRODUCTION TO ITV for primary and secondary faculty, and SECOND CLASSROOM; three each on teaching FOREIGN LANGUAGE, ROLE OF THE CLASSROOM TEACHER, TV AND EDUCATION, and NEW VISION ON TV.

The 1967-68 schedule has six hours of ITV daily: four series at primary levels, 13 at upper elementary, and 11 for junior-senior high, plus in-service series which include LINGUISTICS AND LANGUAGE LEARNING and ROBERTS LANGUAGE series from KQED, San Francisco; ENGLISH: FACT AND FANCY; CANFIELD SPEAKS; the National Council of Teachers of Mathematics series from United World Films; one on Human Relations; and locally produced offerings in Economics, English as a Second Language, PROBLEM TEACHING for elementary grades, SCIENCE TEXT, TECHNIQUE METHODS in Social Studies, and Spanish.

HERITAGE: THE STORY OF SAN DIEGO employs film, graphic, and dramatic components. ART AROUND US is a secondary school Art Appreciation series. COMMUNITY!, for grades 8 and 11 Civics, uses city and county examples of planning, government, fire and police protection. CROSSROADS continues as an experimental series for grades 5-8 on creative reasoning. NEWS OF THE WEEK for grades 4-6 offers depth presentations of State, national and world events.

Of about 30 new instructional programs, six are considered innovative or experimental: in Language Arts MAGIC CARPET for primary grades with contests in writing and art to stir student participation; TODAY IS TOMORROW, two series for grades 8-9 and 10-12 on Vocational Education; PERSONAL DECISIONS for grades 5-12 on Narcotics, Alcohol, Tobacco and other health education matters; and ART AROUND US consists of 20 programs for grades 8-12.

Of San Diego's 57 series being telecast in 1967-68, new ones acquired from outside resources are BOSTON SYMPHONY, DYLAN THOMAS, and MAN IN SPACE for grades 7-12 from Seven Arts; FROM FRANKLIN TO FROST on American Literature for grades 10-12 from MPATI; the ILLINOIS MATHEMATICS FOR THE GIFTED, for grades 4-6, through Great Plains; PROFILES IN LANGUAGE and PROFILES IN MUSIC for grades 10-12 from San Diego State College; ROUNDABOUT for pre-schoolers, from WETA in Washington; STEPPING IN RHYTHM for K-3 from WVIZ, Cleveland; MEET THE ARTS for grades 4-6 from WGBH, Boston; and SPORTSMANLIKE DRIVING for grades 10-12, all through the NCSCTV.

The annual Superintendent's Report has an estimated 5,000 viewers. Special one-time programs in early 1967 were presented on UNDERSTANDING ITV, a preview for parents, DENTAL HEALTH, PHYSICAL FITNESS, and ON LSD TODAY.

Since 1951-52 the city schools' Department of Adult Education has presented TV CLASSROOM on public service time contributed by a commercial station. Peak registration was nearly 200 in 1960-61 until there were marked rises in 1963-64 to over 400, in 1964-65 to over 900, and 1,280 in 1966-67 when the Department began taping its courses in color. Courses are telecast on Saturday mornings from 6:00 to 7:30 and replayed on Mondays, Wednesdays and Fridays at 6:30 a.m. In 1967-68 nine series will be telecast for 10 weeks each: American Literature, California History, Spanish, Modern Mathematics, Geography, Family Relations, American Art, Modern Mathematics (repeat) and General Science.

FACILITIES

The ITVA staff has offices adjacent to the San Diego State College campus. College production facilities included 40' x 50' and 25' x 30' studios, four cameras, three videotape recorders (two of them eight years old), and a film chain. The scene shop is inherited from the college theatre. No remote pick-up facility nor editing equipment were at hand on June 12, 1967, but these additions were anticipated.

San Diego city schools have 210 TV sets in elementary classrooms, 68 in junior high, 53 in senior high schools, 3 as yet unconverted to UHF in its community college, and seven in central offices. 65 more were on order but unassigned in June, 1967.

One high school was equipped with closed-circuit television. Two others were being installed.

The ITVA budget for 1967-68 totals $371,292. The largest item is for Instruction.

SAN FRANCISCO

ITV ORGANIZATION

Educational station KQED provides an ITV service which is organized on a fifteen county basis and which is cooperatively financed by some 120 public school districts and 40 parochial and private schools. There are over 300,000 students and 10,000 teachers using the instructional service this year throughout the region.

The San Francisco Schools participate in this regional organization in two ways: (1) by contracting for its total a.d.a. in grades K-6 (some 56,000 students and teachers); and (2) by joining the BRITE Curriculum Development and Coordinating Agency which is established and supported by the County Superintendent of Schools in the Bay Region.

BRITE employs a professional Executive Director (Dr. Robert Morrill) who, with the assistance of curriculum specialists from the contracting districts, determines the curriculum areas to be developed through instructional television. There are over one hundred district curriculum specialists who work on Subject Area Committees during the school year.

PROGRAMS AND USES

Two-thirds of the ITV programs are produced locally by KQED. The balance is obtained by exchange with other educational stations or by rental through NCSCTV and MPATI. While many of the series have received national recognition, San Francisco teachers with whom we talked said they do not offer much to inner-city children.

YOU AND I, a series of 30 programs on creativity and imagination in art, has been well received in local schools and is being distributed by the National Center for School and College Television.

MATH CLUB sets up problems. Students have worksheets at their desks. The screen goes blank when the time comes for students to perform computation, permitting class involvement in the solutions.

Primary teachers cited as helpful SCIENCE IN ACTION, LET'S FIND OUT (for grade 2) and BAY AREA ADVENTURE.

FACILITIES

KQED has outgrown its present studio location and now occupies three separate buildings to house its staff of 150 employees. The thirty engineers employed are all union members (**nabet**).

Property in San Francisco has been purchased for a new four million dollar studio complex. Estimates are that construction will be completed during 1970. Present facilities are cramped, not sound-proofed and operating out of a building structure that was formerly a warehouse and garage.

Engineering equipment and arrangements are good. Three color Marconi cameras are operative along with three Marconi black-and-white cameras. There is one fully-equipped mobile unit and one-black-and-white unit, also fully equipped. In addition, two separate film crews are available for assignment.

The San Francisco schools have 597 television sets in current school use. At City College of San Francisco there are a closed circuit television studio and tape recording facilities which are used primarily for student training in a wide variety of vocations, including pre-service teacher education.

WASHINGTON, D. C.

ITV ORGANIZATION

District of Columbia Public Schools withdrew from the Greater Washington ETV Association in 1959. In 1967-68 three District Schools will use television on a pilot basis.

In 1966-67 the Association served 18 member school systems which subscribed $1 per pupil in grades 1-6 and $.25 per student in grades 7-12. It operates Channel 26, and has a construction permit for Channel 32 which is expected to be used primarily for secondary school programming and college credit courses for teachers, continuing education for adults, etc.

The Superintendents and Instructional Budget Committee, consisting of Assistant Superintendents and Directors of Instruction, determines financial participation of member schools and subject areas to be offered. The Budget Committee has appointed eight Curriculum Councils with representatives from member districts who determine course content, choose TV teachers, and serve as evaluation committees.

TV teachers receive their regular salaries plus a 5% increment their first year, 10% thereafter; from $3 to $5 per lesson plan; and added pay for further materials such as visuals. Theoretically, they are TV teachers for a maximum of three years, but this limit has not been rigid. 1966-67 was the sixth year for Cynthia Brumback and Mary Janet Blackburn, and the fifth for John N. Robbins, Jr.

In 1966-67 the WETA School Service had a Manager, Assistant Manager who was Field Director, Administrative Assistant, one Program Assistant, and ten Studio Teachers.

PROGRAMS AND USES

WETA produces about four new school series a year. In 1967-68 these will be 30 programs in the COVER TO COVER grade 5-6 Literature series; 20 for UNDER ONE SUN, grade 5-6 Social Studies; 15 Health programs for junior and senior high schools; and 15 FOR THE LOVE OF ART programs for grades 4-6.

Its 1966-67 offerings for K-3 were ALIVE AND ABOUT by Jane B. Cheney of WEDH, Hartford, on wildlife and conservation for grades 2-3; Boston's ALL ABOUT YOU on Health for grades 1-2; ART COMES ALIVE by Cynthia Brumback for grades 2-3; MAGIC OF WORDS by Mr. Robbins for grades 1-3; SHAPES IN SPACE, Geometry for grades 2-3, by Donna Cagey; Boston's SING, CHILDREN, SING with Tony Saletan for grades 1-2; Pittsburgh's TELL ME A STORY by Margaret Hodges for grades 1-2; New York's TIME NOW FOR MUSIC for grades 3-4; and Mary Janet Blackburn in WINDOW ON OUR WORLD, Social Studies for K-2.

Intermediate grade series were New York's AMERICAN HISTORIC SHRINES for grades 4-5; ART WORLDS by Mrs. Brumback for grades 4-6; COVER TO COVER by Mr. Robbins for grades 5-6 and his EXPLORING OUR LANGUAGE for grade 4; INQUIRY INTO LIFE, Life Science for grades 4-6 by Alex Costea; Pittsburgh's PEOPLE AND THEIR WORLD taught by Robert E. Honse, grade 6-7 Social Studies; New York's PLACES IN THE NEWS; Mrs. Judith Searles in READING NEWSPAPERS; and SCIENCE SPOTLIGHT by Tom Cabelus for grades 5-7.

There were also MPATI's FROM FRANKLIN TO FROST, American Literature for senior high schools, and four series for teachers: SETS AND SYSTEMS; ENGLISH: FACT AND FANCY; PARLONS FRANCAIS; and LIVING LANGUAGE (English).

FACILITIES

WETA was enlarging its building and checking out seven new Norelco color cameras in the summer of 1967. Its entire plant is professionally equipped, with Art and Construction departments capable of carrying forward expanded School Television operations.

This station has collaborated in experimental new departures for School Television. Among these have been the planning and production of three programs which attempted to use programmed learning principles for teaching Human Geography, and the pre-school ROUNDABOUT series in cooperation with the United Planning Organization.

APPENDIX E
TELEVISION STATION LICENSEES/GRANTEES and OWNERSHIP CLASSIFICATION
GREAT CITIES 1966-67

STATION	CHANNEL	LICENSEE/GRANTEE and ADDRESS	TYPE OF OWNERSHIP
WGBH-TV	2	WGBH Educational Foundation, 125 Western Avenue, Boston, Massachusetts (02134)	Community
WBGX	44	Same as above	Community
WNED-TV	17	Western New York Educational TV Association, Inc., Lafayette Hotel, Buffalo, New York (14202)	Community
WTTW	11	Chicago Educational Television Association, 5400 N. St. Louis, Chicago, Illinois (60625)	Community
WXXW	20	Same as above	Community
WVIZ-TV	25	ETV Association of Metropolitan Cleveland, 4300 Brookpark Road, Cleveland, Ohio (44134)	Community
WTVS	56	Detroit Educational Television Foundation, Inc., 26945 W. 11 Mile Road, Southfield, Michigan (48075)	Community
KCET	28	Community Television of Southern California, (for Los Angeles), 1313 North Vine Street, Hollywood, California (90028)	Community
WKNO-TV	10	Memphis Community Television Foundation, Box 80,000, Memphis State University, Memphis Tennessee (38111)	Community
WMVS	10	Board of Vocational and Adult Education, 1015 North 6th Street, Milwaukee, Wisconsin (53203)	School
WMVT	36	Same as above	School
WNYE	25	Board of Education, City of New York, 112 Tillary Street, Brooklyn, New York (11201)	School
WHYY-TV	12	WHYY, Inc., 46th & Market Streets, Philadelphia, Pennsylvania (19139)	Community
WUHY-TV	35	Same as above	Community
WQED	13	Metropolitan Pittsburgh Educational Television, 4337 5th Avenue, Pittsburgh, Pennsylvania (15213)	Community
WQEX	16	Same as above	Community
KETC	9	St. Louis Educational Television Commission, 6996 Millbrook Blvd., St. Louis, Missouri (63130)	Community
KEBS	15	Trustees of the State of California, Colleges for San Diego State College, 5146 College Avenue, San Diego, California (92115)	School
KQED	9	Bay Area Educational Television Association, 525 Fourth Street, San Francisco, California (94107)	Community
WETA-TV	26	The Greater Washington Educational Television Association, Inc., 1225 19th Street, N.W. at Jefferson Pl., Washington, D. C. (20036)	Community

STATUS OF ITFS APPLICATIONS AND OPERATIONS IN THE GREAT CITIES (AUGUST, 1967)

NORTHEAST REGION

Chairman — Dr. Bernarr Cooper, Chief, Bureau of Mass Communications, New York State Educational Department, Albany, New York.

APPLICANT, PERMITTEE, OR LICENSEE	CHANNELS	FILED – GRANTED	ON AIR
BOSTON			
Boston Catholic TV Center, Inc. Att. Msgr. Flaherty 25 Granby Street Boston, Massachusetts 02215	D-1, 2, 3, 4 (10w)	6/23/66 – 1/19/67	
Northeastern University c/o Professor Roy Johnston Northeastern University Room 6N Boston, Massachusetts 02115	A-3, 4 (10w)	3/2/67	
BUFFALO – none			
NEW YORK			
Roman Catholic Diocese of Brooklyn Rev. Malloy (Kings County, N. Y.) 75 Greene Avenue Brooklyn, New York 11238	F-1, 2, 3, 4 Cg. to B-1, 2, 3, 4 (10w)	6/5/64 – 7/28/64 7/9/64	4/11/67 (B-1, 2)
Rt. Rev. Msgr. Leonard Hunt 451 Madison Avenue New York, New York Archdiocese of New York, N. Y. (New York County, New York) 10022	A-1, 2, 3, (10w)	8/19/64 – 1/29/64	11/66 (A-1)
See BPIF-9 (for Jamaica, Brooklyn, New York)	C-1, 2, 3, 4 Cg. to F-1, 2, 3, 4	6/5/64 – 7/28/64 7/9/64	4/66 (F-3, 4)
The Roman Catholic Diocese of Brooklyn, New York (See BPIF-9)	CP to replace expired permit	9/29/66 – 1/5/67	
The Roman Catholic Diocese of Brooklyn (See BPIF-10)	CP to replace expired permit	9/29/66 – 1/5/67	
The Roman Catholic Diocese of Brooklyn, New York (See BPIF-9)	F-1, 2, 3, 4 (10w)	1/23/67 – 2/13/67	

PHILADELPHIA* – none
*Philadelphia has prepared a plan for use of ITFS by the Public Schools.

APPLICANT, PERMITTEE, OR LICENSEE	CHANNELS	FILED – GRANTED	ON AIR

PITTSBURGH – none

SOUTHERN REGION

Chairman – William Smith, Director, Mississippi Authority for ETV, P. O. Drawer 2470, Jackson, Mississippi 39205.

BALTIMORE

Rev. Manuel Roman 330 North Charles Street Baltimore, Maryland Roman Catholic Archbishop of Baltimore, Maryland (Baltimore and surrounding counties)	A-1, 2, 3 (10w)	9/10/64 – 12/29/64	

MEMPHIS – none

WASHINGTON, D. C.

Rt. Rev. Msgr. Thomas Lyons Archdiocese of Washington, D. C. Patrick A. O'Doyle, Archbishop 1721 Rhode Island Avenue, N.W. Washington, D. C. 20018	C-1, 2, 3, 4 (10w)	11/15/65 – 7/26/66	

MIDWEST REGION

Chairman – Dr. Robert Shultz, Director of TV, Illinois State Office of Public Instruction, Springfield, Illinois.

CHICAGO – none

CLEVELAND

Rev. Msgr. William N. Novicky Diocese of Cleveland 1027 Superior Avenue Cleveland, Ohio 44113	E-1, 2, 3, 4 Chg. to C-1, 2, 3, 4 (10w)	7/29/65 – 4/29/66	
See BPIF-45, (Cleveland and Shaker Heights, Ohio)	C-1, 2, 3, 4 Chg. to A-1, 2, 3, 4 (10w)	7/29/65 – 4/29/66	
CO-IND-ED (Commercial Industry Education), c/o Harold S. Davis Rockefeller Building Cleveland, Ohio 44113	A-1, 2, 3, 4	9/29/66	
Educational TV Assn. of Metropolitan Cleveland, c/o Louis S. Pierce 4300 Brookpark Road Cleveland, Ohio 44134	G-1, 2, 3, 4 (10w)	1/23/67	

APPLICANT, PERMITTEE, OR LICENSEE	CHANNELS	FILED – GRANTED	ON AIR
Board of Education of the Cleveland City School District, Paul W. Briggs, Superintendent 1380 East 6th Street Cleveland, Ohio 44114	E-1, 2, 3, 4 (10w)	4/11/67	

DETROIT

Archdiocese of Detroit 1234 Washington Blvd. Detroit, Michigan 48226 Rev. Dennis Harrety	A-1 (10w)	12/2/64 – 4/1/65	
Mr. John F. X. Browne Bd. of Education of the City of Detroit 9345 Lawton Avenue Detroit, Michigan (Metropolitan Michigan) 48206	C-2, 3 (20w) Cg. ERP to 10w	4/9/65 – 7/20/65 7/19/65	11/22/65 (C-2, 3)
Wayne State University Dr. James B. Tintera 5035 Woodward Avenue Detroit, Michigan 48202	E-1 (10w)	9/13/66 – 1/5/67	

MILWAUKEE

Marquette University c/o Mr. Raymond T. Bedwell School of Speech 625 North 15th Street Milwaukee, Wisconsin 53233	A-1, 2 (10w)	10/26/66 – 3/20/67	
Archdiocese of Milwaukee Milwaukee, Wisconsin Rt. Rev. Edward J. Gobel 437 West Galena Street Milwaukee, Wisconsin 53212	C-1, 2, 3, 4 (.25w)	4/11/67	
"	G-1, 2, 3, 4 (10w)	"	
"	C-1, 2, 3, 4 (10w)	"	
"	G-1, 2, 3, 4 (10w)	"	
"	C-1, 2, 3, 4 (10w)	"	
"	G-1, 2, 3, 4 (10w)	"	
"	G-1, 2, 3, 4 (10w)	"	
"	C-1, 2, 3, 4 (10w)	"	

APPLICANT, PERMITTEE, OR LICENSEE	CHANNELS	FILED – GRANTED	ON AIR
ST. LOUIS – none			

WESTERN REGION

Chairman – vacant

LOS ANGELES

Archdiocese of Los Angeles Education and Welfare Corp. Rev. John C. Urban 1531 West 93rd Street Los Angeles, California 90047	A-1, 2, 3, 4, Amend to B-1, 2, 3; Chg. Tx. (10w)	9/25/64 – 5/7/65 4/13/65	5/1/67 (B-1, 2, 3)
"	E-1, 2, 3, 4 Amend to G-1, 2, 3 (10w)	9/25/64 – 5/7/65 4/13/65	5/1/67 (G-1, 2, 3)

SAN DIEGO – none

SAN FRANCISCO*

BPIF-91 The Roman Catholic Welfare Corp. of San Francisco Msgr. Francis Quinn 441 Church St. San Francisco, California 94114	G-1, 2, 3, 4 (.25w)	1/23/67	
BPIF-92 (See BPIF-91)	B-1, 2, 3, 4 (10w)	1/23/67	
BPIF-93 (See BPIF-91)	B-1, 2, 3, 4 (10w)	1/23/67	
BPIF-94 (See BPIF-91)	D-1, 2, 3, 4 (10w)	1/23/67	

*San Francisco has initiated a feasibility study on ITFS for the Unified School District.

Key SCHOOL TELEVISION Personnel
in the Great Cities 1967*

BALTIMORE

    School TV   Eleanora Kane, Supervisor
                                  Radio-Television Department
                                  Baltimore Public Schools
                                  Smith Ave. and Greely Road
                                  Baltimore, Maryland 21209

    CCTV   Clay Stall, Supervisor
                                    Instructional Materials Center
                                  Baltimore Public Schools
                                  Eden and Oliver Streets
                                  Baltimore, Maryland 21205

    Community TV   -----

    Community   Eleanora Kane
    Relations

BOSTON

    School TV   -----

    CCTV   -----

    Community TV   Lauriston Ward, Exec. Dir.   Robert L. Larsen, Dir.
                                  Massachusetts Exec. Committee Educational Division, WGBH
                                      for Educational Television   125 Western Avenue
                                  State Department of Education   Boston, Mass. 02134
                                  120 Boylston
                                  Boston, Massachusetts 02116

    Community   Ron Johnson
    Relations   Director of Information
                                  Boston Public Schools
                                  15 Beacon Street
                                  Boston, Massachusetts 02108

BUFFALO

    School TV   Seymour Abeles, Project Administrator of Federal Projects
                                  816 City Hall
                                  Buffalo, New York 14202

    CCTV   -----

*Four areas of responsibility for school television are listed. Of course, in many cases there is an overlap of responsibility.

Key SCHOOL TELEVISION Personnel

Community TV   Anthony Buttino, Director
                    Instructional Broadcasting, WNED
                    Western New York Educational
                       Television Association
                    Lafayette Hotel
                    Buffalo, New York 14202

Community   ————
Relations

CHICAGO

School TV   Carole R. Nolan, Consultant
                       in Charge of Closed Circuit Television
                    Chicago Board of Education
                    228 North LaSalle Street
                    Chicago, Illinois 60601

CCTV   Carole R. Nolan

Community TV   Marge Hopper, Executive Director
                    Chicago Area School Television
                    5400 North St. Louis Avenue
                    Chicago, Illinois 60625

Community   ————
Relations

CLEVELAND

School TV   James Tanner   Ed Potokar, Coordinator
                    Assistant Superintendent   of Instructional Television
                    Cleveland Public Schools   Cleveland Public Schools
                    1380 East Sixth Street   1380 East Sixth Street
                    Cleveland, Ohio 44114   Cleveland, Ohio 44114

CCTV   Ed Potokar

Community TV   Betty Cope, Station Manager   Allan Stephenson, Director
                    WVıZ-TV   Educational Services, WVIZ-TV
                    4300 Brookpark Road   4300 Brookpark Road
                    Cleveland, Ohio 44134   Cleveland, Ohio 44134

Community   ————
Relations

DETROIT

School TV   Ethel Tincher, Director
                    Department of Educational Broadcasting
                    9354 Lawton
                    Detroit, Michigan 48206

Key SCHOOL TELEVISION Personnel

CCTV   Ethel Tincher

Community TV   -----

Community   Mrs. Hazel Trumbell
Relations   Press, Radio & Television Relations
                        Detroit Public Schools
                        5057 Woodward Avenue
                        Detroit, Michigan 48202

LOS ANGELES

School TV   George Lange, Supervisor
                        Radio-TV Section
                        Los Angeles City School District
                        450 North Grand Avenue
                        Los Angeles, California 90012

CCTV   -----

Community TV   Charles Callaci, Coordinator
                            of Educational Services, KCET
                        1313 North Vine Street
                        Hollywood, California 90028

Community   John Gillean, Supervisor
Relations   Public Information Office
                        Los Angeles City School District
                        450 North Grand Avenue
                        Los Angeles, California 90012

MEMPHIS

School TV   Elizabeth Hamlin, Director
                        Elementary Education
                        Memphis City Schools
                        2597 Avery Avenue
                        Memphis, Tennessee 38112

CCTV   -----

Community TV   Fred Willis, Program Director
                        Memphis State University, WKNO
                        Memphis, Tennessee 38111

Community   Robert Simonton
Relations   Director of Public Information
                        Memphis City Schools
                        2597 Avery Avenue
                        Memphis, Tennessee 38112

Key SCHOOL TELEVISION Personnel

MILWAUKEE

School TV
Robert Suchy, Director
Department of Instructional Resources
Milwaukee Public Schools
5225 W. Vliet Street
Milwaukee, Wisconsin 53208

CCTV
————

Community TV
Dr. Otto Schlaak
Station Manager, WMVS & WMVT
1015 North 6th Street
Milwaukee, Wisconsin 53203

Community Relations
William Lamers, Assistant Superintendent
Division of Elementary Schools
Teacher Personnel & Community Relations
Milwaukee Public Schools
5225 W. Vliet Street
Milwaukee, Wisconsin 53208

NEW YORK

School TV
James Macandrew, Director
Educational Radio & Television, WNYE
112 Tillary Street
Brooklyn, New York 11201

CCTV
Hal Marder

Community TV
————

Community Relations
Jerome G. Kovalcik, Director
Office of Public Relations
Board of Education of the
  City of New York
110 Livingston Street
Brooklyn, New York 11201

Joy Fisher, Coordinator
Radio & TV
Office of Public Relations
Board of Education of the
  City of New York
110 Livingston Street
Brooklyn, New York 11201

PHILADELPHIA

School TV
Martha Gable, Director
Instructional Materials Division
Philadelphia Public Schools
Parkway at 21st Street
Philadelphia, Pennsylvania 19103

Nina Hink, Asst. Director
Radio-Television
Philadelphia Public Schools
Parkway at 21st Street
Philadelphia, Pennsylvania 19103

CCTV
————

Community TV
Bruce Beale, Program Director
WHYY
4548 Market Street
Philadelphia, Pennsylvania 19139

Key SCHOOL TELEVISION Personnel

Community   Joseph L. Pollock, Director
Relations   Information Services
                         Philadelphia Public Schools
                         Parkway at 21st Street
                         Philadelphia, Pennsylvania 19103

PITTSBURGH

School TV   Charles Hettinger, Associate Director
                          of Learning Resources for Radio and
                          Television Education
                         Pittsburgh Public Schools
                         341 South Bellefield Avenue
                         Pittsburgh, Pennsylvania 15213

CCTV   ----

Community TV   Rhea Sikes, Director
                         of School Services, WQED
                         4337 Fifth Avenue
                         Pittsburgh, Pennsylvania 15213

Community   Dorothea Pefferman, Assistant Director
Relations   Information Services & Community Relations
                         Pittsburgh Public Schools
                         341 South Bellefield Avenue
                         Pittsburgh, Pennsylvania 15213

SAN DIEGO

School TV   Stephen A. All, Manager   William Stegeman, Asst. Supt.
                          Instructional Television   in charge of Curriculum Devel.
                          SDA/ITVA   San Diego City Schools
                          5164 College Avenue   4100 Normal Street
                          San Diego, California 92115   San Diego, California 92103

CCTV   James Hilgen
                         Samuel F. B. Morse High School
                         San Diego Unified School District
                         6905 Skyline Drive
                         San Diego, California 92114

Community TV   John Witherspoon, General Manager
                         KEBS-TV
                         5164 College Avenue
                         San Diego, California 92115

Community   ----
Relations

Key SCHOOL TELEVISION Personnel

SAN FRANCISCO

School TV
Dr. Joseph Hill
Coordinator of Curriculum
San Francisco Unified School
  District
135 Van Ness Avenue
San Francisco, California 94102

Dr. William Sanborn
Director of Instructional Materials
San Francisco Unified School
  District
135 Van Ness Avenue
San Francisco, California 94102

CCTV
Henry Leff, Director
Radio-TV
City College of San Francisco
San Francisco, California 94112

Community TV
Dr. Robert E. Morrill
Executive Secretary
Bay Region Institutional Television for Education (BRITE)
County Government Center
590 Hamilton
Redwood City, California 94063

Raymond L. Smith
Director of School Broadcasts,
  KQED
525 Fourth Street
San Francisco, California 94107

Community
Relations
Hugh E. Wire, Supervisor
Educational Information
San Francisco Unified School District
135 Van Ness Avenue
San Francisco, California 94102

ST. LOUIS

School TV
Dr. Earl Herminghaus, Director
Division of Curriculum & Educational
  Research
3026 Laclede Avenue
St. Louis, Missouri 63103

CCTV   ----

Community TV
Robert C. Glazier, Exec. Director
KETC
6996 Millbrook Boulevard
St. Louis, Missouri 63130

Basil Murray, Director of School
  Services
St. Louis Public Schools
911 Locust Street
St. Louis, Missouri 63101

Community
Relations
Elaine D. Afton, Director
Community Relations Division
Board of Education of the City
  of St. Louis
911 Locust Street
St. Louis, Missouri 63101

Key SCHOOL TELEVISION Personnel

WASHINGTON, D. C.

    School TV   ----

    CCTV   ----

    Community TV   Mrs. Mary Jane Phillips, Manager
                                    School Television Services, WETA
                                    2600 Fourth Street, N.W.
                                    Washington, D. C. 20001

    Community   ----
    Relations

APPENDIX F
STATEMENT OF CHARLES BENTON, PRESIDENT
THE FUND FOR MEDIA RESEARCH

Before House Committee on Interstate and Foreign Commerce During Hearings on the Public Broadcast Act, July, 1967

MR. BENTON. Thank you, Mr. Chairman.

Mr. Chairman, I am grateful for this opportunity to testify on the Public Broadcasting Act. My remarks are based on experience in private business in the development and production of educational films as former president of the Encyclopaedia Britannica Educational Corp. and of Encyclopaedia Britannica Films.

Today I appear in my capacity as president of the Fund for Media Research, a private, nonprofit foundation engaged in a study of the status and needs of instruction, as served by television, in 16 major cities.

The fund is conducting this study on behalf of the Research Council of the Great Cities Program for School Improvement. The membership of the Council includes 16 major metropolitan school districts involving around 4 million youngsters, or roughly 10 percent of the total school population in the United States.

My comments are based on direct knowledge of the uses of modern audiovisual techniques in improving classroom instruction.

I would like to express my full support for the goals of the legislation now before this committee. A sound program of public television can be a force for improving the quality of all television, and indirectly the advancement of education.

My comments today concern one specific section of this bill, Title III, which authorizes a study of instructional television which may cost as much as $500,000. While the idea of a Government-supported study is good, I am concerned that Congress makes the purposes quite clear, so that the result can be as authoritative and useful as the Carnegie Commission report.

I believe the study proposed by Title III can be extremely useful if it is expected to provide the Congress, the educational community, and private business with clear answers they need to aid in the most productive development of instructional television.

But to get any such answers, we must first ask the right questions. I think that the committee might find it impractical — as did Senator Pastore's subcommittee in the Senate — to rewrite section 302. Yet either through language in the bill itself or through a clear statement in the committee report, the Congress should state what it feels the character of these questions should be.

In my view, quite aside from the important topics given as examples in section 302, dealing with content of the study, there are some vital matters the study plan should consider essential. I respectfully ask if the six examples in section 302 indicate how the study should tie directly to our most pressing educational needs.

H.R. 10408, conforming H.R. 6736 as adopted by the Senate, omits this description of content. When witnesses suggested changing in its phrasing, Senator Pastore said that details should be left to the Secretary of Health, Education, and Welfare.

It was prudent of the Senate to delete that section. It would be desirable to make clear possibly in your report to the Congress your realistic and practical intent in authorizing Title III in three respects. The points I submit all apply to the urgent, unmet needs of the disadvantaged children in our inner cities.

If taken into account, they would also serve large numbers of other students in public and private schools throughout the Nation.

It is not absolutely certain that the Title III study will put the most pressing needs of pupils and teachers first, nor that it will come to grips with city problems that Dr. Conant has called social dynamite.

No matter what else this study does, if it were not to examine inner-city requirements it will be remiss. Now, to three factors that deserve emphasis:

First, what is instructional television? What does it do? The Title III research should start with basic needs of education. Among the conditions we are seeing on our study of instructional television in the Big Cities is the high turnover of pupils and teachers. In some schools well over 100 percent of the children move in and out per year. Thousands speak not English, but a dialect or only a foreign language. In language ability, thousands enter the first grade a year behind the norm, and by the sixth grade are as many as 4 years behind. Arithmetic skills show the same dismal pattern.

There is the absence of motivation with more than half of all students dropping out along the line before high school graduation in some large cities. More than 6,000 teachers in New York City alone were newly hired last year. Most have no inner-city teaching experience, and the teacher preparation program for such teachers is almost nonexistent.

We are seeing how television can mitigate these enormous problems. Chicago has devised clusters of schools linked by closed circuits. These are financed under Title III of the Elementary and Secondary Education Act. Much of the pupil turnover is within a neighborhood cluster. When a child moves to another school with the same television teachers, there is less dislocation.

In Detroit, one new child — now in her fourth school that same year — was unreachable by any teacher until she saw the TV screen and exclaimed, "There's my teacher!"

Many superintendents have told me that a major advantage from television is inservice teacher training. We are seeing school systems where telecast series provide the framework for updating what is taught and how it is taught, particularly in the sciences and with math concepts still new to the teachers, who were raised on the "old math." In some cities television series on "Human Relations," aimed primarily at the teacher, have provided a useful stimulus for the frank discussion of problems in this area.

However, too often television offerings are mere supplements. We find them largely incidental decoration, remote from what schools must do. As one superintendent put it, "TV hasn't in any way done anything but supplement the traditional."

Seldom do we find enough programs for children at markedly different levels of achievement, designed for their individual aptitudes, interests, and problems. The potentially powerful tool of television can offer the good teacher a wide repertory to draw upon, as her students require.

In order to meet the special instructional needs of the inner city, the school broadcast efforts of the community station are not sufficient. The big-city schools also need their own narrowcast facilities — CCTV, 2,500 megacycles — to handle their own critical requirements.

Second, what national policies can encourage better ITV programming for improving learning? The Title III study should explore ways the Federal Government can encourage private risk investment.

Surely, the best professional resources of the educational publishing and audio-visual industries ought to be available, producing materials that educators can draw upon. Even though the need is evident, there is no market. Why? Risks are costly and they must be balanced against a chance for reasonable profits.

ITV was born with foundation money as an experiment, but the experiment is over. ITV is now a reality in American education that needs competitive quality programming. Educators should be able to select for their schools' needs from competitive sources. I neither underestimate the problems nor know the answer in school television. But one can be found that will protect the public interest and will advance instructional results.

Third, the country needs to learn more than "whether Federal aid for instructional media is proper and what form it should take." The Title III study should estimate the scale of financing necessary to use instructional television well, much as the Carnegie Commission did in projecting public television costs.

To duck this question would be to risk drifting into multi-million-dollar expenditures in taxpayers' money on half-measures not worth buying.

Let me amplify each point briefly and suggest that in the long run Title III can be as important as any authorization the Congress has ever made to strengthen education in this Nation.

First, the new media can be centrally constructive instead of on the "enrichment" fringes. While instructional television is not now generally making a major contribution to better teaching and learning, virtually all of the administrators and curriculum people we are talking to in the Big Cities agree that its potential is enormous.

Further, they seem to appreciate the uncommon work being done by resourceful instructional television supervisors and staff who cope, often superbly, with insufficient time, people, and money. What they have in abundance are courage, energy, and fine working relationships. To date, however, most boards of education and key administrators have not assigned high priority commitments to the electronic agents of change.

The Carnegie Commission observed that "instructional television has never been truly integrated into the educational process," that — like educational radio and films — it has been "put to incidental and occasional uses as ancillary material."

There are isolated contrasts. In May, I visited American Samoa with a group of Big-City school superintendents. There we saw television instruction at the heart of an entire school system. How much greater the potential should be in the 50 States.

Both John Goodlad, of UCLA, and Father John Culkin, of Fordham University, remind us that this year's high school graduate has, on an average, had 12,000 hours of classroom instruction, but has watched 15,000 hours of television.

Without neglecting logistics, the Title III study should recognize the "electronic upbringing" of the generation now at school, whose members have watched television since they were weaned. The flow of signals is as normal to them as air and water. It is unfortunate that nobody knows how our educational system can mobilize the full power of this medium for better teaching and learning of today's "television generation."

My second suggestion is to attract private competitive investment. The incomparable wealth of vivid material being developed by the foremost textbook publishers and educational film producers is rarely used on -- or in conjunction with — school television.

As a former producer of films which school systems buy widely, I know that very few of our films were being telecast. There is something wrong when teachers use printed descriptions and line drawings of cell division when their students could see through microphotography this life process itself; when at the flick of a switch they can watch distant lands and peoples, or the reenactment of memorable statesmen and great events from the past.

School and community stations assembling lessons find it easier to restrict content to what is at hand. They lack time and money to cull from film libraries and graphics collections, and to arrange for clearances. There isn't any visible market for the education industries, even for excerpts of their products over television.

More and more major companies have been entering the education field. None that I know of is making any serious investment in instructional television programming, where their professional resources could be invaluable. The uncertainties on copyright further inhibit risk capital as well as the maximal use of existing visual materials. Title III represents an opportunity to lay the groundwork for the resolution of this impasse.

Lastly, the scale of resources — in money, personnel, facilities, and time — needed to get really substantial benefits from the new media must be anticipated. The Carnegie Commission deferred examination of instructional television, recommending the study proposed in Title III. It reported that there is as yet no basis for making cost estimates in the manner projected for public television.

Congress should consider requesting that the Title III study seek cost criteria in terms of instructional effectiveness, to find out what kind of money will be necessary to meet the priority needs of students and teachers. Unless we learn this, money spent meagerly could be largely wasted because we would get little for it.

In our inner-city slums, we are finding that even record-high per-pupil expenditures bring poor results, unless there are resources enough to accomplish the relevant tasks. It is the same principle as the critical mass required to set a chain reaction into motion.

There are times when we need to remind ourselves of what we already know. At the risk of belaboring the obvious, in the phrase "instructional television" the more important word is "instructional." The ultimate in engineering design cannot make up for poor teaching.

The Title III study must regard advancing technology as a means, never an end. Television and other electronic media are still a new set of instruments. At their best, they are simply tools. The technological factors ought never be permitted to eclipse our concentration on primary goals. And the most important of these is the better teaching and learning for all the children in our fast-changing society.

THE CHAIRMAN. Thank you, Mr. Benton.

Mr. Moss, have you any questions?

MR. MOSS. Mr. Chairman, I would just like to make an observation that I have made earlier.

In the course of authorizing the study, this committee has to take cognizance of the jurisdictional allocations made under the Reorganization Act of 1946. We can create problems on the floor of the House which can damage or defeat legislation if we go beyond the scope of the jurisdiction of this committee.

Some of the recommendations you have made in your statement, while excellent, while worth while in every respect, would, in my judgment, place this committee on a collision course with the Committee on Education and Labor. I think the price we would pay under those conditions would be far too great to hazard the risk.

The answer certainly should be sought and every effort should be made to gain the cooperation of the Committee on Education and Labor to see that some of the specific items mentioned are studied. But in the broader sense, this is the Committee on Interstate and Foreign Commerce and is concerned with broadcasting. That is where we gain our jurisdiction.

If we start getting into the more narrow field of closed circuit and then the general overall problems of the adequacy of instruction, the problems of teacher turnover or student failure, we are treading on very tender toes that sometimes react with great vigor on the floor of the House.

I merely wanted that made clear in the record.

THE CHAIRMAN. Mr. Brotzman?

MR. BROTZMAN. I would like to thank the gentleman for his statement. I have no questions, Mr. Chairman.

THE CHAIRMAN. Mr. Benton, I want to thank you, too. We are glad to have had you with us. You follow a long parade of distinguished Americans who have appeared here in behalf of this legislation.

As Mr. Moss has said, we agree it is an excellent statement, with worthwhile objectives. I am sure that the Congress will take cognizance of what you have said. You have added to the record.

I agree with Mr. Moss that some of these questions would perhaps raise some jurisdictional problems, but we will take those into consideration.

Thank you again for coming before the committee.

MR. BENTON. Thank you so much. It is a real problem that Congressman Moss has mentioned. I hope that some real thought will be given as to how to intermesh these forces. It is something that has to be faced if the full potential is to be realized.

Thank you.

APPENDIX G

PERSONS AND SOURCES HELPFUL TO THIS STUDY

Without the responsive cooperation of hundreds of Great City school personnel who were interviewed, and who patiently provided further information upon request, this inquiry would be without substance or validity.

The Fund for Media Research is also indebted to many other generous individuals outside the school systems. Space forbids a complete roster. Among the officers of government agencies, universities, independent schools, foundations, corporations, educational and professional associations who furnished advice and information were:

John Anderson
Ampex Video Institute
Elk Grove Village, Ill.

Benjamin Barnett, Jr.
Arthur D. Little, Inc.
Cambridge, Mass.

Dr. Richard H. Bell
Ampex Corporation
Redwood City, Calif.

Hon. William Benton
Encyclopaedia Britannica
New York, N.Y.

Miss Virginia Biggy
Assistant Superintendent of Schools
Concord Public Schools
Stow Street
Concord, Mass. 01742

Dr. Thomas A. Billings
Office of Economic Opportunity
Upward Bound
Washington, D.C.

Charles Bowen
Booz, Allen & Hamilton
Chicago, Ill.

Frederick Breitenfeld
Maryland-Educational Cultural Television
Baltimore, Md.

Gertrude Broderick
United States Office of Education
Washington, D.C.

Mr. Vernon Bronson, Director
Office of Research & Development
NAEB
1346 Connecticut Avenue, N.W.
Washington, D.C. 20036

John Bystrom
TV Consultant
Dept. of Health, Education & Welfare
Washington, D.C.

Judith Cauman
Head Start
Office of Economic Opportunity
Washington, D.C.

Tom Clemens
United States Office of Education
Washington, D.C.

Edward Cohen
National Center for School & College Television
Bloomington, Indiana

Donald Cook
Radio Corporation of America
New York, N.Y.

Father John Culkin, S.J.
Fordham University
New York, N.Y.

Rev. Michael J. Dempsey, Asst. Supt.
Catholic Schools Office
75 Greene Avenue
Brooklyn, N.Y. 11238

Richard Dienhart
Instructional Television
New Trier High School
Winnetka, Ill.

Peter Dirr
WNDT
New York, N.Y.

Robert Dressler
Ampex Video Corporation
Elk Grove Village, Ill.

Don Ely
Syracuse University
Syracuse, N.Y.

Dr. Alvin C. Eurich
Academy for Educational Development, Inc.
1180 Avenue of the Americas
New York, N.Y.

Alan Fink
T.V. Director
Pasadena P.S.
351 South Hudson
Pasadena, Calif. 91109

James Fitzpatrick
Arnold & Porter
Washington, D.C.

Scott Fletcher
Executive Consultant
NAEB
1346 Connecticut Avenue., N.W.
Washington, D.C. 20036

Ray Fry
United States Office of Education
Washington, D.C.

Dr. Lawrence Frymire, Exec. Director
Illinois Telecommunications Commission
State of Illinois Bldg., Room 2102
Chicago, Ill. 60601

James Gibson
National Archives
Washington, D.C.

Irving Gitlin
Irving Gitlin Productions
New York, N.Y.

Brother Robert Godfrey
Archdiocese of St. Louis
St. Louis, Mo.

Morton Goldsholl
Morton Goldsholl Associates
Northfield, Illinois

Dr. John Goodlad
University of California
Los Angeles, Calif.

Ronald Gross
Academy for Educational Development, Inc.
1180 Avenue of the Americas
New York, N.Y.

Charles C. Halbower
Arthur D. Little, Inc.
Cambridge, Mass.

Mr. William Harley, Pres.
NAEB
1346 Connecticut Ave., N.W.
Washington, D.C. 20036

Robert Hilliard
Federal Communications Commission
Washington, D.C.

Anna Rosenberg Hoffman
Anna M. Rosenberg Associates
New York, N.Y.

Delayne Hudspeth
Syracuse University
Syracuse, N.Y.

Dr. Anna L. Hyer
Executive Secretary
DAVI
1201 Sixteenth St., N.W.
Washington, D.C. 20036

Ran Ide
Ontario Department of Education
Ontario, Canada

Philip Jackson
University of Chicago
Chicago, Ill.

Richard Jaffee
Office of Economic Opportunity
Washington, D.C.

Irving Kassin
Chicago, Ill.

John C. Kennan
Society for Visual Education
Chicago, Ill.

Ben Kubasik
National Citizens Committee for Public Schools
New York, N.Y.

Dr. Norton Kristy
Technomics, Inc.
Santa Monica, Calif.

Herman Land
Herman Land Associates
New York, N.Y.

Governor Rex Lee
American Samoa
Pago Pago

Claire List
The Ford Foundation
New York, N.Y.

Rt. Rev. Albert W. Low
Archdiocese of Boston
Boston, Mass.

Borden Mace
Sterling Institute
Boston, Mass.

Leonard Marks
United States Information Agency
Washington, D.C.

Michael Maloney
Encyclopaedia Britannica Educational Corp.
Chicago, Ill.

Mr. Carl L. Marburger
Assistant Commissioner of Education
Bureau of Indian Affairs
1951 Constitution Ave., N.W.
Washington, D.C. 20240

Harold Mayer
Mayer Products, Inc.
New York, N.Y.

Sterling McMurrin
University of Utah
Salt Lake City, Utah

Edward Meade
Ford Foundation
New York, N.Y.

Richard J. Meyer
WNDT TV
New York, N.Y.

Newton Minow
Chicago, Ill.

Lloyd M. Morriset
Carnegie Corporation
New York, N.Y.

Robert Morrison
Chicago, Ill.

Judith Murphy
Academy for Educational Development, Inc.
1180 Avenue of the Americas
New York, N.Y.

Dr. Carroll Newsom
Radio Corporation of America
New York, N.Y.

Walter M. Noel, Jr.
Arthur D. Little, Inc.
Cambridge, Mass.

Steven Ocko
United States Information Agency
Washington, D.C.

Elsa Parrott
National Counsel Associates
Washington, D.C.

Robert Pirsein
Instructional Television
New Trier High School
Winnetka, Ill.

Frances Plude
Archdiocese of Boston
Boston, Mass.

Elias Porter
Technomics, Inc.
Santa Monica, Calif.

Don Quayle
Eastern Educational Network
Boston, Mass.

Robert Reed
Hawaiian Educational TV
Honolulu, Hawaii

Lewis Rhodes, Director
Project for Instructional Development
NAEB
1346 Connecticut Ave., N.W.
Washington, D.C. 20036

Mary E. Robinson
Office of Economic Opportunity
Washington, D.C.

Maurice Rosenblatt
National Counsel Associates
Washington, D.C.

Joe Russin
Public Broadcast Laboratory
New York, N.Y.

Lowell Sachnoff
Chicago, Ill.

Ole Sand
National Education Association
Washington, D.C.

Donald L. Sandberg
Director of Field Services
National Center for School & College Television
Bloomington, Indiana

Robert Saudek, Director
NYU Institute of Film & Television
New York University
New York, N.Y.

Monsignor Ralph R. Schmit
Archdiocese of Milwaukee
Milwaukee, Wis.

Wilbur Schramm
Palo Alto, Calif.

Gene Schweck
Danforth Foundation
St. Louis, Mo.

John Sessions
Washington, D.C.

Leonard Schrager
Chicago, Illinois

Dr. Robert Shultz
State Department of Public Instruction
Springfield, Ill.

Paul Schupbach
Great Plains ITV Library
Lincoln, Nebraska

Robert Snider
National Education Association
Washington, D.C.

Harold Spears
San Francisco Board of Education
San Francisco, Calif.

Ray Stanley
United States Office of Education
Washington, D.C.

Edmund Stephan
Chicago, Ill.

George Stevens, Jr.
American Film Institute
Washington, D.C.

Herbert A. Thelen
University of Chicago
Chicago, Ill.

I. Keith Tyler
National Project for Improvement of Televised
    Instruction
Ohio State University
Columbus, Ohio

Larry Van Murek
Communication Films
Los Angeles, Calif.

Don White
National Audio Visual Association
Fairfax, Va.

Dr. Harvey White
Hall of Science
University of California
Berkeley, Calif.

John White
National Educational Television
New York, N.Y.

Mr. Lee Wickline
Director of Title III
U.S. Office of Education
Washington, D.C. 20202

Mr. Harold Wigren
Educational Television Consultant
NEA
1201 Sixteenth Street, N.W.
Washington, D.C. 20036

Dr. Lawrence H. Wilsey
Booz, Allen & Hamilton
Chicago, Ill.

Dr. Burton R. Wolin
Technomics, Inc.
Santa Monica, Calif.

None of these friends shares responsibility for the Report's accuracy, interpretation, and judgments. The Fund welcomes viewpoints which differ with its findings, from them and from others. The immediate future of urban education is too important to lose out on any gains that may come from the clash of opposing convictions and ideas.

APPENDIX H

SCHOOL TELEVISION: GREAT CITIES 1967

A DISCUSSION & DEMONSTRATION VIDEOTAPE

The work being done in School TV by the Great Cities during 1966-67 included many interesting facts and program concepts. Many of the facts can be found in the printed report "School Television: Great Cities 1967." Human and visual elements of School TV cannot be conveyed well enough by any written report. Some direct exposure to the programming itself is desirable. This is why The Fund for Media Research selected samples of programming showing the four major uses of School Television and assembled a representative group of persons from the Great Cities to discuss School Television in 1966-67. The panel discussion and excerpts from some of the programs were recorded on videotape.

I. Introduction

    A. Dr. Sidney P. Marland, Jr., Superintendent of the Pittsburgh Public Schools and President of the Research Council of the Great Cities Program for School Improvement, discusses the background and purpose of the School Television Study. Charles Benton, President of The Fund for Media Research, summarizes the major findings of the Study and introduces the panel.

    B. The panel has a representative from each of the seven professional groupings interviewed during the course of the Study. They are:

    Mr. Steve A. All, Director, Instructional Television, San Diego Area/Instructional Television Authority.

    Dr. Carl Byerly, Associate Superintendent, Detroit Public Schools.

    Dr. Bernard Donovan, Superintendent of Schools, Board of Education of the City of New York.

    Mrs. Georgiana Hardy, President of the Board of Education, Los Angeles

    Dr. Marita Hogan, Principal, Richard E. Byrd Elementary School, Chicago.

    Mr. Frank Mesiah, former teacher and Audio-Visual Director, now Assistant Director of Integration, Buffalo Public Schools.

    Mr. Robert Petza, Elementary Teacher, Baltimore Public Schools.

Mr. Benton reviews the eight most acute instructional problems as defined by school people in the 16 cities. These were:

    1. Curriculum relevance and diversity

    2. Teacher quality and quantity

    3. Interfering environmental realities

    4. Excessive teacher load

    5. Poor communication among administrators, teachers, parents and children

    6. Administrative leadership and practices

    7. Insufficient and/or unpredictable financial support

    8. Inadequate facilities

II. The School Television Excerpts

These illustrate the four uses of School Television.

A. DIRECT INSTRUCTION

1. "Mr. Whatnot" from WNED-TV, Buffalo, teaches language and reading skills adapting a format proven popular with young children.
2. "Art For You" produced by WVMS, Milwaukee. The works of great artists are discussed on TV and also are available as inexpensive color reproductions in classrooms.
3. "Demand Performance," a program shown twice weekly to Pittsburgh Public Schools over WQED. Those films for which there is highest demand on the audio-visual list are telecast.
4. "Places in the News," from the new Public School TV station WNYE, New York. Current events, and personalities associated with them, are presented. Questions from viewers are answered on the program.
5. "Process to Product," produced by the SDA/ITVA and telecast over KEDS, San Diego. This experimental series uses the inquiry approach to stimulate creative thinking and develop problem-solving skills.

B. TEACHER EDUCATION

6. "English — Fact and Fancy" produced by WETA, Washington, D.C. It is a nationally-syndicated teacher-education series which examines the English language as a living instrument rather than as an abstract system of communication.
7. "Human Relations," one of several such programs produced in the Great Cities, is from WHYY of Philadelphia. Teachers receive background information regarding social change and cultural differences through discussions by experts of national prominence.

C. ADMINISTRATIVE

8. "Hard Times and Great Expectations." Dr. William Kottmeyer, Superintendent of St. Louis Public Schools, uses the commercial TV stations to deliver his annual report to the school staff and community.
9. "LSD Today." This program, involving the local student government, was prepared and presented in 72 hours by the SDA/ITVA to communicate to city school students, staff, and parents the nature and dangers of LSD.

D. COMMUNITY INFORMATION AND EDUCATION

10. "Modern Math for Parents." At the request of the local PTA, the Detroit Public Schools presented this explanatory series on "new" math concepts to parents over Station WTVS.
11. "Robinson Reports." Presented over WVIZ-TV, Cleveland, this program adopts the commercial approach to the late evening interview show as a platform for an open discussion of problems and accomplishments in Project Head Start.

III. Panel Discussion

The discussion following the excerpts probes the needs for building-level CCTV systems, good local programming, better utilization and evaluation, the use of TV for teacher training and adult education, and copyright problems. Student involvement in TV, the use of outside experts, and TV's immediacy in communicating with students, staff, and community are discussed. Finally, the panel suggests that:

1. The Great Cities should cooperate in producing programs that each can use.

2. New techniques of programming should be explored.
3. Curriculum and TV people should work together.
4. Teacher-training institutes should help strengthen pre-service training in the uses of television.

It is hoped that this videotape can be useful to individual cities, along with the written report, as a springboard for discussion in staff meetings of cities interested in applying the findings of the report.

We are particularly grateful to the Ampex Corporation and the New Trier Township Instructional Television Department for their invaluable technical support. Hopefully, this initial effort will inspire other television programs on the creative uses and potentials of School Television in Great Cities' schools.

BIBLIOGRAPHY

Any problem for which no answer is known has a vast literature. A complete bibliography on urban schools and instructional television would require thousands of entries. This annotated listing reports on those sources which were especially helpful to those who made this Study.

GENERAL

John I. Goodlad, *The Changing School Curriculum,* New York, Fund for the Advancement of Education, 1966.
> The best current comprehensive survey of the aims, methods, materials, and status of the important new curricula in Science, Math and the Humanities. Helpful commentary and short bibliography.

Parents' Reactions to Educational Innovations, Gallup International, Inc., Princeton, N. J., 1966.
and
School Board Members' Reactions to Educational Innovations, Gallup International, Inc., Princeton, N. J., 1966.
> Two opinion studies, under a Kettering Foundation grant, measure attitudes from a wide geographic cross-section obtained by grid samples presumably following accepted polling techniques. The main finding of the first study is that parents are more ready to welcome innovation than most educators appreciate. For example, independent study was approved by 93%, and team teaching by 84% of the parents.
> The second poll found that school board members approved the same two proposals by 59% and 88%. Questionnaires and statistical breakdowns are included.

Francis Keppel, *The Necessary Revolution in American Education,* New York, Harper and Row, 1966.
> Historical development of public education as background of current problems. Discusses programs seeking to modernize and improve school practices. Eleven charts and eighteen tables present national data.

Peter Schrag, *Voices in the Classroom,* Boston, Beacon Press, 1965.
> A reporter looks at public schools in eight geographic areas. Chicago and San Francisco are among them. Others range from Newton, Mass. and Jefferson County, Colo. to Appalachia.

TEACHER EDUCATION

Herbert Schueler and Gerald S. Lesser, *Teacher Education and the New Media,* Washington, D.C., American Association of Colleges for Teacher Education, 1967.
> A critique of media research related to teacher education, based on 467 study reports, articles, and books, directing attention to needs for more rigorous research which can establish clearer standards of teaching performance, gain more basic understanding of teaching and learning processes, and develop more effective means of producing teacher competence.

Stanford University, *Micro-Teaching: a description,* School of Education, Stanford, mimeographed, 1967.
> Papers on four years' work with micro-teaching. Interns teach 5 to 20 minute lessons to a group of 4 or 5 high school students. Lessons are recorded on video tape. Students criticize, then interns and supervisors review comments and the taped lesson prior to having the intern reteach a revised lesson to a different group. Summer clinics use this to improve seven teaching skills, and with team teaching of larger "micro-classes". Project has developed an appraisal guide as test instrument. Clinics produce significant behavioral changes in teaching candidates.

THE DEPRIVED

Carl Bereiter & Siegfried Engelmann, *Teaching Disadvantaged Children in the Preschool,* Englewood Cliffs, N. J., Prentice-Hall, Inc., 1966.
> Depth study of pilot pre-school program for disadvantaged children. Stresses need for language-skills training to permit successful primary school experience. Describes specific classroom techniques.

Benjamin S. Bloom, Allison Davis and Robert Hess, *Compensatory Education for Cultural Deprivation,* New York, Holt, Rinehart & Winston, 1965.
> Report derived from Research Conference on Education and Cultural Deprivation at University of Chicago, June, 1964. Summarizes current knowledge about problems of educating the deprived, with broad yet specific recommendations. Annotated bibliography of 108 articles and books.

James S. Coleman et al., *Equality of Educational Opportunity*, Washington, D. C., National Center for Educational Statistics, U. S. Office of Education, 1966.
> A report to the President and Congress on the lack of equal educational opportunities in public education. Exhaustive data on segregation, school offerings, and the relationship of school resources to pupil achievement. Reproduces tests and questionnaires prepared by the Educational Testing Service.

Milly Cowles (ed.): *Perspectives In the Education of Disadvantaged Children*, New York, World Publishing Co., 1967.
> Fourteen papers sympathetically analyze medical, cultural, educational, and social deficits of inner-city children, for teachers and volunteers.

Lester D. Crow, Walter I. Murray & Hugh H. Smythe, *Educating the Culturally Disadvantaged Child*, New York, David McKay Co., 1966.
> Sociological text for pre-service course. Seeks to give student teachers a sympathetic understanding of the inner-city school child and his learning problems. Selections from several Great Cities' reports outline special programs for the disadvantaged.

Joe L. Frost and Glenn R. Hawkes (eds.), *The Disadvantaged Child*, Boston, Houghton, Mifflin Co., 1966.
> Anthology of readings from professional and lay journals by 57 authors describes problems, experiments and programs.

Robert E. Herriott and Nancy Hoyt St. John, *Social Class and the Urban School*, New York, John Wiley & Sons, 1966.
> Using data developed through the National Principalship Study at Harvard (1958 et. seq.), this is a useful restudy of attitudes toward urban children. Awareness of conflicting values is one important basis of a considerable array of compensatory and remedial activity since source data were gathered.

Joseph O. Loretan and Shelley Umans, *Teaching the Disadvantaged*, New York, Teachers College Press, 1966.
> A compendium of new approaches — with 33 exhibits — presented as guidelines "by and for school people" for formulating programs.

Charles Mitchell, *The Culturally Deprived: Educating the Disadvantaged*, Chicago, Research Council of the Great Cities Program for School Improvement, 1964.
> Explains, with examples, the background, scope and urgency of a major problem with which the Research Council is concerned. Directed to the public-at-large.

National Council of Teachers of English, *Language Programs for the Disadvantaged*, Champaign, Illinois, 1965.
> Twenty-two active members of the NCTE spent three months visiting 115 school districts, and met with consultants to plan and write this stimulating report. Touching programs which go from Head Start to adult education levels across the country, they pinpoint and discuss strengths and weaknesses of compensatory education. Recommendations follow each section. More and less effective techniques are described in sufficient detail to convey practical caveats to persons involved in inner-city education.

National Education Association, *Education and the Disadvantaged American*, Washington, D. C., 1962.
> A primer on the causes, problems and requirements of the deprived. Nothing in this pamphlet will come as news to Great City school people.

A. Harry Passow (ed.), *Education in Deprived Areas*, New York, Teachers College Press, 1963.
> Seventeen contributors present papers on facets of inner-city schooling. Psychological and sociological patterns of student problems, programs, school organization, and teacher orientation.

Research Council of the Great Cities Program for School Improvement, *Instructional Materials to Meet the Needs of Urban Youth*, Chicago, 1965.
> Guidelines for selection of reading and teaching materials needed in inner-city schools.

Racial Isolation in the Public Schools, Washington, D. C., 1967. U. S. Commission on Civil Rights, (U. S. Government Printing Office).

    Study of the extent and effects of segregated schooling nationally. Various attempted solutions — bussing, pairing, compensatory programs, desegregation, supplementary centers, magnet schools, educational parks are examined. Recommendations.

    Volume 2, Appendices, contains "Working Papers": *"The School Park",* by John H. Fischer; *Desegregating the Integrated School* by John I. Goodlad; *Educational Technology in the Educational Park* by Francis Keppel; *Towards Educational Equality* by Dan C. Lortie, and *Desegregation Techniques* by Neil V. Sullivan.

Michael Usdan and Frederick Bertolaet (eds.), *Teachers for the Disadvantaged,* Chicago, Follett Publishing Co., 1966.

    Reports of three task forces requested to describe satisfactory teacher performance in depressed urban areas, teacher education curricula likely to encourage comparable performance, and the identification of criteria for measuring successful teacher education programs. A Great Cities Research Council project.

CRITICISM OF SPECIFIC SITUATIONS

Marilyn Gittell, *Participants and Participation, A Study of School Policy in New York City,* Center for Urban Education, 1967.

    Report of a study under an OEO contract analyzes and condemns decision-making in New York City schools; the roles of community groups, teachers' union, Board of Education, and administration. Recommends weaker administrative powers for central staff, and expanded influence of Mayor, political, parent, and neighborhood organizations. Proposes a detailed reorganization plan.

Peter Schrag, *Village School Downtown,* Boston, Mass., Beacon Press, 1967.

    Censures Boston public schools, blaming political, economic and sociological factors affecting inner-city education.

EDUCATIONAL TELEVISION

Carnegie Commission on Educational Television, *Public Television, A Program for Action,* New York, Harper & Row (hard cover), Bantam Books (paperback) 1967.

    The basis for the Public Broadcasting Act of 1967. Concludes that "a well-financed, well-directed" ETV system, "substantially larger and far more pervasive and effective ... must be brought into being if the full needs of the American public are to be served."

    Distinguishes between public TV, directed to the general public, and ITV, dealing primarily with formal instruction, but considers "these two parts as constituting a single whole." Ducks ITV, asking for further study. Recommends that "federal, state, local and private educational agencies sponsor extensive and innovative studies intended to develop better insights into the use of television in formal and informal education."

National Center for School and College Television: *One Week of Educational Broadcasting,* Bloomington, Indiana, 1966.

    Surveys of all U. S. educational telecasts from April 17 to 23, 1966, divided by stations, times, viewers, and subject categories. Measures general, school, college and adult instructional telecasting separately and in sum.

INSTRUCTIONAL TELEVISION

Lee E. Campion and Clarice E. Kelley: *A Directory of Closed-Circuit Television Installations in American Education with a Pattern of Growth,* Washington, D. C., Department of Audiovisual Instruction, National Education Association, 1963.

    Headlong progress has long outdated this publication as a directory. Its perspective papers by Harold E. Wigren, ETV Consultant to NEA, and co-author Campion, Section III on Facilities and Equipment, Utilization, and Study Findings are most valuable.

John E. Lynch et al (eds.): *Radio and Television in the Secondary School,* Bulletin of the National Association of Secondary School Principals, vol. 50, no. 312, Washington, D. C., October, 1966.

    Papers by 42 experienced authorities. A treasury of practical information and thoughtful discussion. Bibliography and periodical list.

Attitudes Toward Instructional Television, report prepared for the Ford Foundation, New York, International Research Associates, 1965.

    Interviews with 26 administrators, 54 TV teachers, 103 classroom teachers, 351 students (and 78 parents) in Washington County, Maryland, Detroit Public Schools, Chicago City Junior College, and the University of Texas.

    Found public school administrators think benefits of ITV outweigh "losses caused by the impersonal character" of TV, that above- and below-average students get a better education with TV than from traditional classroom schooling. Classroom teachers and parents find TV makes school more interesting but creates frustrations, problems of group discipline and individual self-discipline. Parents believe the quality of TV teaching is superior to that of most classrooms.

National Program on the Use of Television in the Public Schools: *Reports on the first, second and third years; Some Reflections on the First Year,* and *Teaching by Television,* New York, Ford Foundation, 1958-61.

    Establishes that children learn by TV, which is "essentially neutral. It can transmit the bad as well as the good, the mediocre as well as the superior." TV is useful for team teaching, with skills of many teachers used in planning and presenting courses, and for in-service training. Historically important. Much of content now, with hindsight, seems quaint.

Kenneth J. Lenihan, Herbert Menzel, and Sydney S. Spivack, *Utilization of the Regents Educational Television Broadcast Programs,* New York, Bureau of Applied Social Research, Columbia University, 1963.

    Estimates 1,400,000 program exposures (some pupils watching more than one program) week of April 2-6, 1962. Science programs most popular. Use in 45% of elementary, 19% of secondary schools. 9% of New York City public elementary schools used Regents programs, 30% in New Jersey, 17% in Connecticut. Catholic schools showed greatest use in Newark, most classes watching 2 to 5 programs a week. Obstacles were poor reception, lack of sets, "inadequate room or spacial arrangements", bell schedules. Of 9,000 to 45,000 adult viewers, 98% were women, mostly homebound with small children, one-sixth college graduates.

Jack McBride, *The Twenty Elements of Instructional Television,* Washington, D. C., National Association of Educational Broadcasters, Monograph Service, Issue 1, 1966.

    The founder of the Great Plains ITV Library and General Manager of KUON-TV at the University of Nebraska makes a distillate of his exhaustive experience. Highly specific check-list approach to analysis of educational need, personnel, planning, facilities, maintenance, supplementary materials, feedback, and evaluation.

Wilma McBride (ed.), *Inquiry: Implications For Televised Instruction,* Washington, D. C., National Education Association, 1966.

    Selections from papers and discussion at symposium held at Stephens College. Analyses of role of inquiry in classroom learning and how ITV can promote it. Present use of ITV is seen as one-way introduction of data. Asserts need is for its flexible use to stimulate two-way process of inquiry. Large claims for an experimental ITV series using programmed learning approach.

Judith Murphy and Ronald Gross, *Learning By Television,* New York, Fund for the Advancement of Education, 1966.

    Cites successes, failures, and possible future developments. Urges more flexibility and imagination for ITV to fulfill its considerable potential.

Closed-Circuit Television: A Report of the Chelsea Project, New York City Board of Education, 1962.

    A pilot project, supported by the Ford Foundation and the New York City Board of Education, was jointly undertaken by the Board of Education, the Hudson Guild Neighborhood House, and Language Research, Inc. of Harvard University. Programs were beamed to P.S. 33 (K-6) and the residents of a nearby public housing unit. It lasted from November, 1957 through June, 1961, aiming "to raise the sights of a neighborhood and its public school" in a largely Puerto Rican area.

    This detailed history and evaluation chronicals enough difficulties, disappointments, and achievements to be useful to any city contemplating community-school closed-circuit telecasts.

J. Christopher Reid and Donald W. MacLennan, *Research In Instructional Television and Film,* Washington, D. C., U. S. Office of Education, Bureau of Research, 1967.

    Abstracts of most of 333 research studies, with introductory review of trends by Leslie P. Greenhill.

Wilbur Schramm, *New Educational Media in Action: Case Studies for Planners, I,* Amsterdam, UNESCO, 1967.

    Studies of ITV in American Samoa, Hagerstown, (Maryland), Japan, and radio in Australia, Thailand, and India. Each section describes needs which prompted use of the medium, organization of system, cost, facilities, and personnel, and lessons learned from the experience.

Wilbur Schramm, Philip H. Coombs, Frederich Kahnert & Jack Lyle, *The New Media: Memo to Educational Planners,* Amsterdam, UNESCO Institute for Educational Planning, 1967.

    Based on USIS contract research, discusses problems new media are being used to solve, how effective they are proving to be, how they are used, their cost, and planning for their use.

I. Keith Tyler, *Instructional Television and Radio in the Detroit Public Schools, Survey and Recommendations,* Columbus, Ohio, 1967.

    Survey group of ten studied evolution of radio and TV in Detroit public schools, their evaluation in 1966, future plans, needed facilities and equipment, organizational structure, CCTV and relations of Department of Educational Broadcasting to MPATI and WTVS Foundation.

    Recommended reorganized educational broadcasting center within larger Department of Instructional Media, cooperative production involving adjacent school systems and agencies such as MPATI, scale of fees for outside use of broadcasts, leasing of recorded series to other cities, and continued support of Detroit TV Foundation and MPATI with proviso the latter "re-institute new, quality production for the future."

ITFS, Instructional Television Fixed Service – What it is . . . How to Plan, published by The Division of Educational Technology, National Education Association, for the FCC Committee for the Full Development of the Instructional Television Fixed Service, 1967.